THE
HEALTH READER

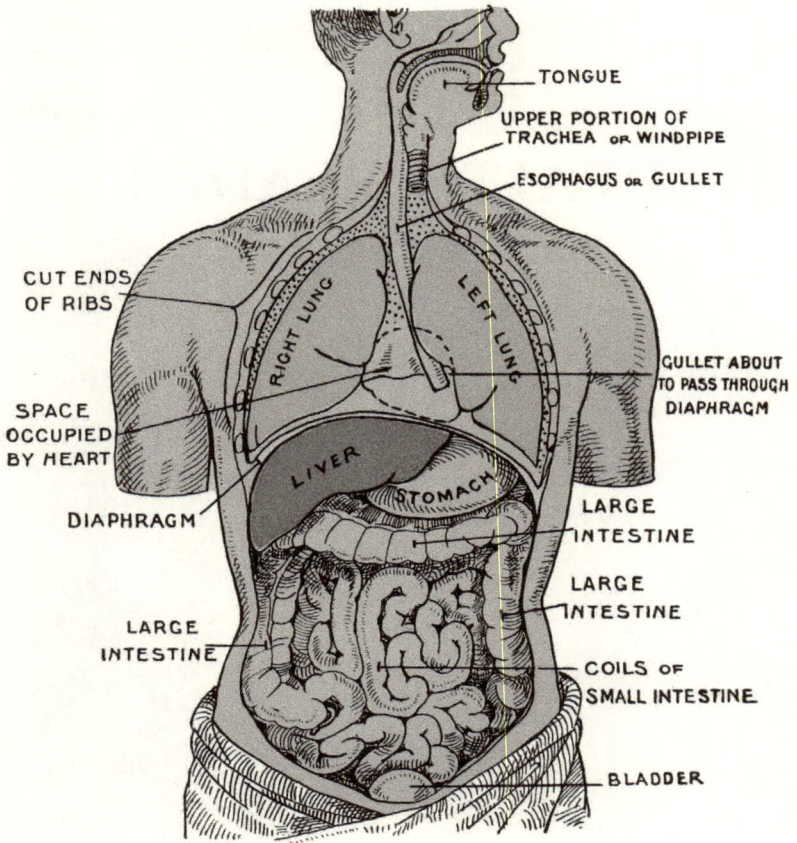

Labels on the diagram:

- TONGUE
- UPPER PORTION OF TRACHEA OR WINDPIPE
- ESOPHAGUS OR GULLET
- CUT ENDS OF RIBS
- RIGHT LUNG
- LEFT LUNG
- GULLET ABOUT TO PASS THROUGH DIAPHRAGM
- SPACE OCCUPIED BY HEART
- LIVER
- STOMACH
- DIAPHRAGM
- LARGE INTESTINE
- LARGE INTESTINE
- LARGE INTESTINE
- COILS OF SMALL INTESTINE
- BLADDER

PLATE I — CHIEF PARTS OF THE HUMAN BODY

THE
HEALTH READER

by

W. Hoskyns-Abrahall

YESTERDAY'S CLASSICS

ITHACA, NEW YORK

This edition, first published in 2021 by Yesterday's Classics, an imprint of Yesterday's Classics, LLC, is an unabridged republication of the text originally published by Cassell and Company, Limited in 1909. For the complete listing of the books that are published by Yesterday's Classics, please visit www.yesterdaysclassics.com. Yesterday's Classics is the publishing arm of Gateway to the Classics which presents the complete text of hundreds of classic books for children at www.gatewaytotheclassics.com.

ISBN: 978-1-63334-151-7

Yesterday's Classics, LLC
PO Box 339
Ithaca, NY 14851

CONTENTS

CHAPTER I

THE HUMAN BODY

"Know thyself: that is the beginning of wisdom."

You will see by the title of this book that it is meant to give some account of health.

This is a subject about which we all ought to know something. Happiness and success in life depend very largely upon health but no one can take proper care of his own health, nor yet of any other person's, without understanding a little about the structure of the human body and the laws of its working. We ought to be at least as ready to learn about this, and to follow scientific methods of treating the body, as we are to adopt improvements in machinery or lighting or means of communication.

You will notice as you read that something is said about animals in this book. The reason is that a study of animals has been one of the principal means by which men of science have arrived at their present knowledge concerning the laws of life. In very many cases what is learnt about animals applies equally to us. In other cases a knowledge of animals has served to lead up to further discoveries which concern humanity alone.

1

You will find two or three instances in the course of the following chapters which will show you what I mean; and I hope you will find very many more for yourselves in your own later reading.

It is not wonderful that it should be so. We and they are all made of the same stuff; and life in all of us is supported by the same means.

First and foremost, we all alike depend upon the **sun**. We could none of us exist without his heat, nor without his light; nor without the water which he draws up for us from the vast surface of the sea nor yet without the winds, caused by him, which bear this water in clouds and shed it on the earth as rain. In a sense we may all well be called children of the sun and it is hardly to be wondered at that in ancient and more ignorant days the sun was worshipped as a god.

As we need sunlight for our very existence, so also we need it for our health—and that most especially when we are young and growing.

In the next place we know that living creatures are constantly taking up into themselves, from the water or from the air, the gas which we call **oxygen**. That is to say, we all **breathe**. We shall see more fully what this means in a later chapter.

Yet again, all living things take up into themselves certain other substances from outside them in the form of **food**. Their bodies have the power of changing this food first into new living substance, and then into those special and different substances of which each creature is composed. Thus the food of a plant becomes in the

2

end wood or leaves, petals or juicy fruit; and the food of an animal becomes shell or bone, flesh, hair, or skin, as the case may be. Your food becomes the different parts of you, and mine of me.

I hope that later on many of you will learn something more of the nature of living substance. In these pages I may only tell you that in itself it is a kind of colourless jelly, to which the name of **protoplasm**, or "first stuff," has been given. It is found chiefly in the form of small roundish bodies which are called **cells**.

Cells

Now every part of every plant or animal begins by being a cell or a group of cells. Some cells are so minute that they can only be seen under microscope lenses of very high power; others may be easily examined. Cut open an orange or a lemon—choose an old one if possible—and observe the little bags in which the juice is held. These are cells. They have been much flattened by being so squeezed together, and the juice which they contain is not protoplasm, but a substance made by protoplasm still, you will be able to understand somewhat how cells are arranged by looking at them.

There are great numbers of plants and animals which consist of only a single cell. There are also plants and animals formed of cells united together, yet resembling one another, each cell doing the same work as all the rest.

Division of Labour among Cells

But the bodies of all the plants and animals we see around us are formed of great multitudes of cells, which have divided among themselves the different kinds of work necessary for the life of the plant or animal.

Thus, in a rose plant some of the cells are altered in one way to make the stem, others are altered in another to make the roots, others make the leaves, the thorns, and the flowers. Again, in a bird some of the cells make the bones, others the flesh, others the skin with its feathers—and so on, of all the parts of the body of the bird.

When a number of cells are thus grouped all together to do the same work they make what is called a **tissue**. So in plants we have leaf-tissue and woody tissue; and in animals we may have bone-tissue, muscle-tissue, and so on. We also speak of the **organs** of breathing or digestion or sense, and by an organ we understand a particular part of the body, composed perhaps of more than one kind of tissue, which does some special work that no other part can do. Thus, for example, we can only see with the eye, our organ of sight, and think with the brain, our organ of thought.

I am sure you will agree with me that there is nothing more wonderful than this division of labour among the cells, and the alterations made in them in order to fit them for their particular work.

The food of every living creature goes, of course, to increase and to renew the cells which form the different tissues of its body. In youth especially the multiplication of cells goes on with extreme activity, and by degrees makes the parts of each creature larger and stronger than they were at first, until at last a certain limit is reached. Then the creature has, as we say, done growing—has arrived at its full size and strength.

This much is true of both plants and animals. We know, however, that between these two kingdoms of life there are many and great differences and it is just in this matter of food that we find the greatest difference of all.

A plant is able to take the substances it needs as food straight from the soil, the water, and the air, and then convert them into living substance.

An animal cannot do this. Beyond taking in air and water it can only use as food substances which have already been changed from non-living into living matter: that is to say, an animal can only be fed upon plants or upon the bodies of other animals.

If you reflect a moment you will see that the animal kingdom, as a whole, depends for its food on the plant kingdom as a whole.

Perhaps you will say: All animals do not eat plants; some eat other animals. But the animals which serve as food were themselves fed on plants; thus a fox may eat a rabbit, but the rabbit feeds on the leaves of plants. So after all we get back to the plant again.

Muscle and Bone Cells

Seeing that we ourselves belong to the animal kingdom, we will now turn our attention to it more particularly.

The food of an animal is usually more difficult to obtain than that of a plant, hence the greater number of animals have to move about and hunt for it.

Now among the powers possessed by living substance is the power of drawing together, or contracting, and then of spreading out again, or expanding.

In the division of labour of which I told you it often happens that some cells give up this power, it being unnecessary for the particular part they have to play. But in the bodies of animals we find that great numbers of cells devote themselves entirely to developing it. They form masses of tissue whose one business in the body is to contract and expand, and it is by means of these movements that the body of the animal, as a whole, is enabled to move.

Such masses of tissue are, as you, know, called **muscle**. In some lowly animals, muscular tissue is the hardest part of the body, and gives it both its shape and its power of movement, as you may see in an earthworm. In the higher animals we find the cells building up a harder tissue, to which the muscles are then attached. This gives the whole body much greater firmness.

In some animals the hard tissue forms the outer covering and protection of the body, as in insects, crabs,

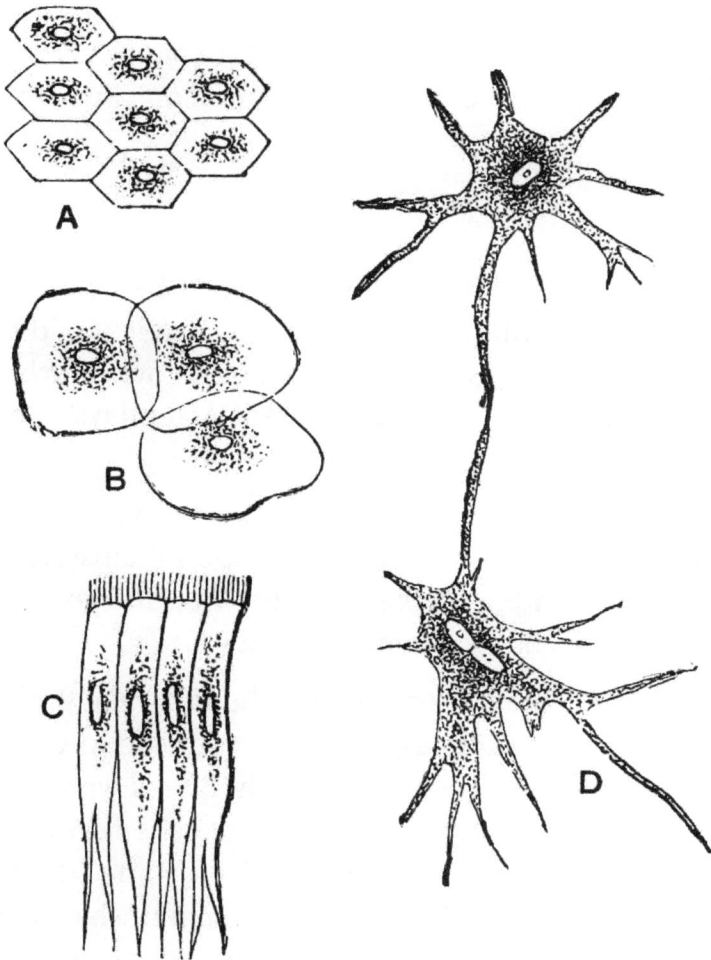

FIGURE 1 — DIFFERENT KINDS OF CELLS

*A, cells from the mucous membrane; B, cells from the lining
of the mouth; C, ciliated (hair-like) cells from wind pipe;
D, nerve cells.*

and lobsters. In the highest animals, the vertebrates
or backboned animals, to which we ourselves belong,
the hard tissue, called **bone**, is inside, and forms a
framework and support to the body.

The muscles and bones of animals are often, as you know, wonderfully strong, and capable of very swift movement. I need not remind you of any instances of this.

Nerve Cells

But you will readily understand that it would be of little use for an animal to be able to move swiftly if it had no means of perceiving where its food was, and of choosing in which direction to move.

And so we find that in all but the very lowliest animals certain cells have taken upon themselves the work of attending to the world outside, and governing the movements of the animal accordingly.

Such cells are scattered over the surface of the body in the lowlier animals, and they correspond to what, in ourselves, is the sense of touch. But as we advance to the higher animals we find these cells beginning a division of labour among themselves. Some, grouping themselves in one place, give the animal what we call the sense of smell; others in the same way bring about the sense of taste; others, again, grouped together in a certain position, bring about the senses of sight and hearing. Besides all these there are many which are stationed, as it were, in the muscles of the animal's body, and start and direct their movements. All these cells are called **nerve-cells**. The most important nerve-cells are those which, in the fore-part, or head, of the bodies of the higher animals, form a mass called the **brain**. The brain is the centre of government for the whole body. It receives messages from the nerves of the senses, and sends orders to the nerves in the muscles, along strands of tissue formed by the nerve-cells for this purpose.

Of all the wonders of protoplasm none is greater than the wonder of the brain and nervous system of animals.

I can only mention it briefly here, just in order to show you in outline how the movements of animals are directed; we shall learn a little more about it later on.

Food-pipe and Blood-vessels

Besides these tissues of muscle and bone and nerve, we find, in all but the very lowliest animals, that some of the cells have formed themselves into a kind of food-bag or food-pipe; into this the food is sent to be made liquid and ready to nourish the tissues.

We also find channels or pipes formed by the cells, by which the liquid food is conveyed round and round the body, so that every part may be supplied.

In a great number of animals the muscular tissue forms a little pump in one part of the channel, and pushes along the liquid which bears the food, We call this pump the **heart**, and in the higher animals the liquid containing the food is known as **blood**.

The Build of the Body

Although it is perfectly true that all living things, and more especially all animals, are our relations, yet, as you may have supposed, some are much nearer relations than others. Of the two great divisions of the animal world—the backboneless or **invertebrates**, and the backboned or **vertebrates**—we belong to the latter and among these again we belong, of course, to the **air-breathers**.

You will find it very interesting to make a list of all the vertebrate animals you know, and then try to sort them out according to the resemblances you notice between them, and guess which are most nearly related to which. The more you are able to study their different shapes and the build of their bodies, the more plainly you will see that they are all made, as it were, upon one great general plan, which has been altered in details to suit different needs, but in essentials remains the same. Here, however, we have only space to consider what is the build of our own body.

We have, as you know, a head, a trunk, and two pairs of limbs. These are supported and held together by a bony framework or **skeleton** within us. In this we may notice first of all the **backbone** or **vertebral column** (Figure 2), from which the vertebrates receive their name. It is composed of a number of small bones, or **vertebræ**, of a peculiar form, so held together, one upon the other, as to form a column. These vertebræ are separated from one another by discs of gristle

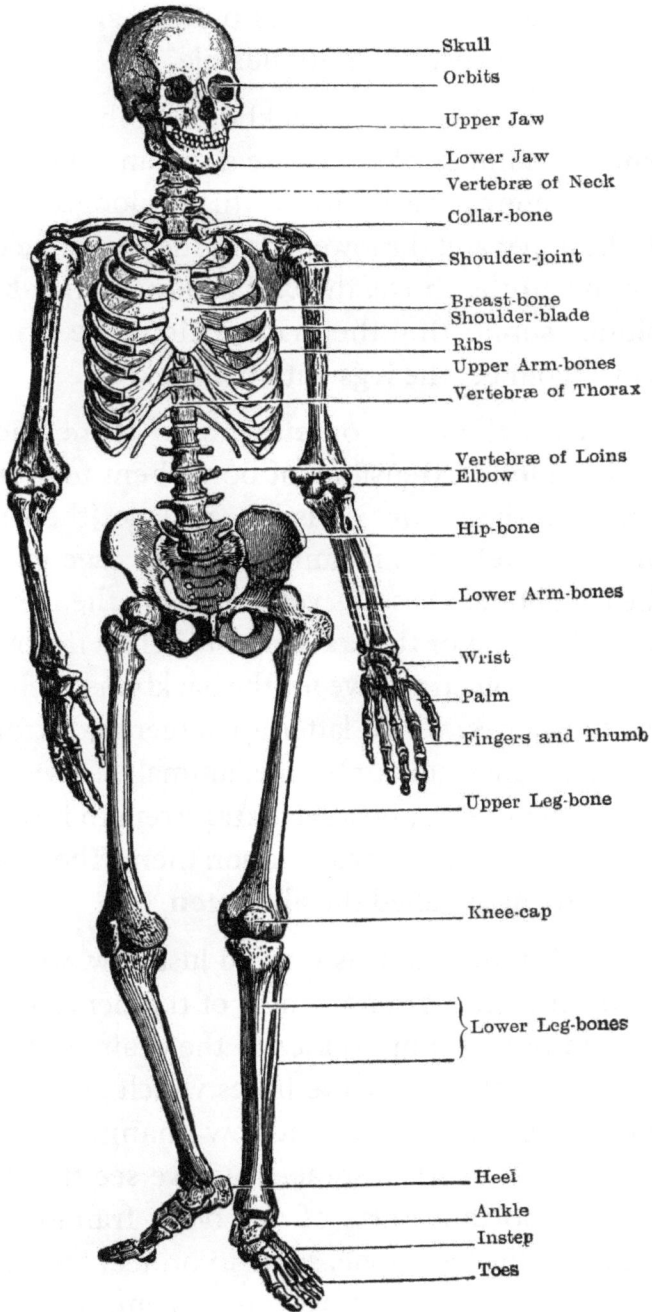

Skull
Orbits
Upper Jaw
Lower Jaw
Vertebræ of Neck
Collar-bone
Shoulder-joint
Breast-bone
Shoulder-blade
Ribs
Upper Arm-bones
Vertebræ of Thorax

Vertebræ of Loins
Elbow

Hip-bone

Lower Arm-bones

Wrist
Palm
Fingers and Thumb

Upper Leg-bone

Knee-cap

Lower Leg-bones

Heel
Ankle
Instep
Toes

FIGURE 2 — THE HUMAN SKELETON

or **cartilage**, which serve as buffers, and render the column to a certain extent flexible.

On the top of the backbone we have the **skull**, where a number of bones are so arranged together as to form a great case, within which is lodged the brain. At the upper and the lower end of the backbone we have a bony girdle: above, the **collar-bones**, and **shoulder-blades** supporting the **arms**; below, the **hip-bones**, which connect the **legs** with the backbone.

Below the neck, on either side of the backbone, we have long extensions of bone, bent forward, and joined at their front ends by cartilage (the so-called **breast-bone**), thus forming a sort of cage in front of the backbone. These, as you know, are the **ribs**, which form the **chest** or **thorax**. Below the chest the trunk has no bony protection save for the backbone itself and for the hip-bones, which latter are larger and stronger in us than in many of our brother animals. This is because, owing to our erect posture, extra strength is needed to support the weight thrown upon them. The lower part of the trunk is called the **abdomen**.

Within the skull, as we said just now, we have the brain, the great ruling centre of the nervous system. Second only in importance to the brain is the **spinal cord**, consisting of nerve fibres which go right down the backbone within a hollow channel formed by openings in the vertebrae. Thus we see that the two most important parts of our bony framework, the skull and the backbone, serve to protect the two most important parts of the nervous system, the brain and the spinal cord.

In the head we have the eyes, ears, nose, and mouth, that is to say the principal **sense-organs**. There also is the upper opening of the **food-pipe**.

In the chest we have the **heart**, the **lungs**, and upper portion of the **food-pipe**.

In the abdomen we have chiefly the **food-pipe**, and the organs which assist it in its work. With these are also other organs, whose business is to help in getting rid of waste matters from the body.

This framework and these organs, when they are full-grown and well nourished, may be of great size, strength, and activity, as we know. What we do not know so well, or perhaps do not always remember, is that they are for the most part slow in reaching their full growth, and during the growing time are not as strong as they will be by and by. Things that happen to them during that time will affect them more, whether for weal or for woe, than things that happen later on. Therefore it is during our youth that a reasonable care will do most good, and unfortunate mistakes work most harm.

While we are still quite little we have to be entirely cared for by older people but as we grow old enough to think and reason we begin to take the care of our own bodies more and more into our own hands. And therefore, let me repeat, it is very necessary that we should learn something about our own structure as soon as we can properly understand it, so that we may be saved from making mistakes which perhaps cannot be repaired when we are fully grown up.

CHAPTER II

THE FOOD-PIPE

*"There are some of our natural desires which only remain
. . . as means of the higher powers acting."*

— Coleridge

We have now learnt a little about the substance of which
plants and animals are made. We have seen, among
other things, that in order to live and grow, plants and
animals must constantly take into themselves matter
from outside.

The matter we take in is, of course, our food and, as
we know very well, we put our food into our mouths,
and swallow it down into a food-pipe, which runs right
through our bodies, and has an opening at the lower
end.

The food-pipe of a man is of what we may consider
a moderate length, neither so short as that of the flesh-
eating or carnivorous, nor so long as that of the herb-
eating or herbivorous animal. Yet perhaps, after all, you
will find it longer than you had supposed when I tell
you that its length, in a man of average height, is about
26 feet. The greater part of it is arranged in a closely-
packed coil which lies in the abdomen.

You will naturally ask why it is necessary that the food-pipe should be so long as this. It is necessary partly because each different sort of food has to be broken up and dissolved in a different part of the pipe, and in rather a different manner and partly because, as you will see, the longer the pipe, the more certainly every bit of good that is in the food will be got out of it and passed into the body.

For you must be careful to remember that the food which is in the food-pipe is not yet in the body: the pipe in itself is nothing but a passage down which substances from outside may be sent.

How the Food-pipe is Made

Let us now consider how this pipe or tube is made. It is composed of muscle, and is lined with a coating of what appears to be an exceedingly delicate and soft skin, which, when examined closely, is seen to consist of a layer of cells that make within themselves a rather thick slimy substance. This substance the cells pour out upon the surface of the food-pipe, and thus keep it smooth and slippery. The word **membrane** is used as the name for a very thin skin; and on account of the slime or **mucus** this membrane is called the **mucous membrane**. The mucous membrane of the food-pipe begins at the mouth and goes the whole way down to the end.

Throughout all the food-pipe run an immense number of tiny blood-vessels, finer than hairs. You cannot see them except by means of a very strong lens, but every part of the food-pipe, and more especially its inner coating, is quite thickly covered with the network they make.

When we examine the food-pipe of some lowly animals, such, for instance, as a worm, we find that the tube is straight, and also that throughout it is of the same width, more or less. But when we come to the higher animals we find that this is not so. Not only is the food-pipe coiled, as we saw above, but we find it stretched out in more than one place so as to form a kind of pocket or bag. This is made possible by the fact that the food-pipe is exceedingly elastic, stretching and contracting very easily. It has been stretched to form a kind of bag in those places in which it is necessary for the food to remain for some time, namely, the mouth, where the food stays for a minute or two, and the stomach, where it stays for three or four hours, and sometimes even much longer. Though it does not form a pouch again the pipe becomes very much bigger round towards the end. By the time the food gets as far as this it has had nearly everything that is useful extracted from it, so that the last part of the food-pipe, while it takes up whatever good is left, is also to some extent a place in which the rubbish is collected until the moment comes for casting it out.

If you will now look attentively at the accompanying diagram (Figure 3) you will see how the food-pipe is arranged. You must not suppose that within the body it looks exactly like this, for a diagram is not so much

CUT END OF GULLET
ENTERING STOMACH

FIRST PART
OF SMALL
INTESTINE

LARGE INTESTINE

LARGE INTESTINE

COILS OF SMALL
INTESTINE

VERMIFORM
APPENDIX

RECTUM

ANUS

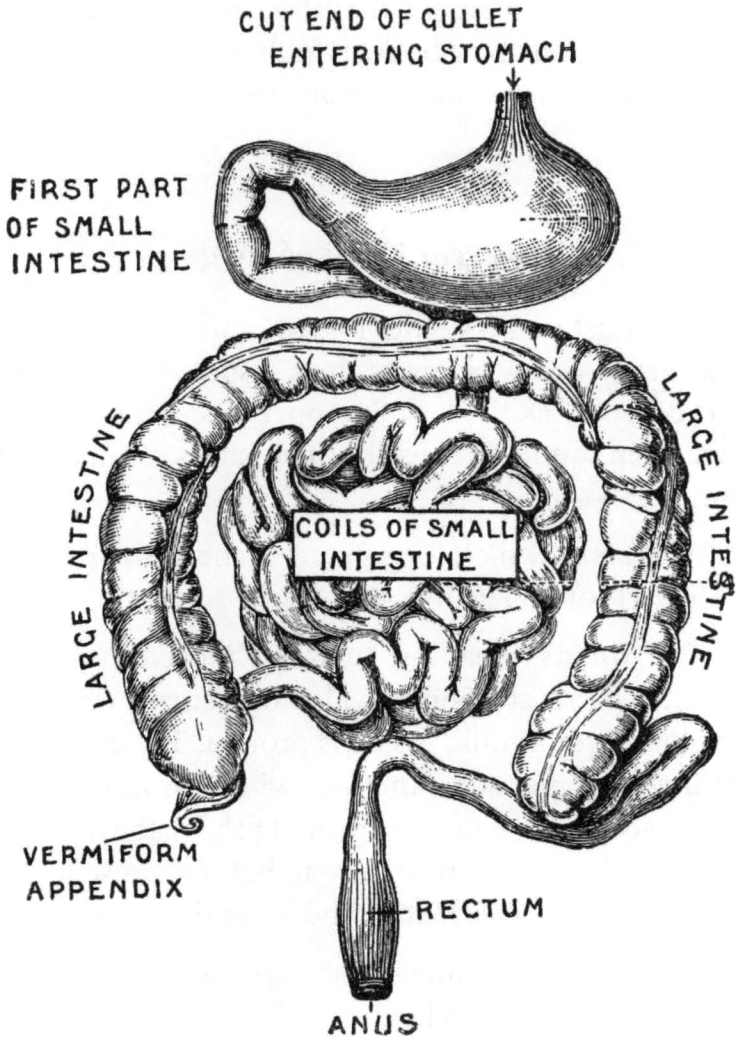

FIGURE 3 — DIAGRAM OF FOOD-PIPE

a picture as a map, designed principally to show the position of different parts with regard to other parts.

You will naturally ask how all this long pipe is kept in place. It would take too long to tell you in detail, but you may remember that it is suspended, chiefly from the region of the back, in folds of membrane. This membrane is exceedingly thin and yet most marvelously strong.

Different Kinds of Foods

We must now consider for a moment the foods we commonly use. Various as their taste is to our sense, and different as they are in appearance, these foods have been found to consist of five kinds of substance. They are:—

1. **Water**—which forms a part (and usually a very large part) of every food-stuff.

2. **Proteins** (meaning "first " or "most important")—which we might perhaps also call **curds**, after the familiar curd of milk, which is protein. These contain **all** the principal substances of which protoplasm is composed. Lean of meat, eggs, and fish are the forms of food which contain most protein but it is present also in milk, bread, peas, lentils, and several other things.

We should remember that water and proteins are absolutely essential to life.

3. **Fats**—substances which burn readily and give us heat, but contain only a part of the material of living substance, or protoplasm. (Examples: butter, milk, fat of meat, bacon.)

4. **Starches and Sugars**—which also burn readily and also contain only certain parts of the material of protoplasm. These are furnished chiefly by our vegetable food.

5. **Mineral matters** or **salts**.

In the chapter on Food you will find a fuller account of these substances; I will only mention here that they are often found together in what may appear to us to be all one kind of substance. Thus milk, besides a very large proportion of water, contains fat, protein, sugar, and salts. The fat collects on the top of standing milk, forming what we call cream.

Proteins, starches, sugars, and fats are nourishing food-stuffs; but, besides the foods which contain them in abundance, it is necessary to eat fruit and green vegetables, which are nearly all water and give us very little actual nourishment. These are wholesome: firstly, because of the water in them; secondly, because they have within them certain salts, dissolved out of the earth by the plants, which are of great service in keeping our bodies healthy; and, lastly, because, as you will see, they are an immense help to the food-pipe in the work it has to do.

In considering food-stuffs you must remember that some proportion of most of them, as we commonly see them and use them, is neither protein, nor fat, nor starch, properly speaking, but is a sort of wrapping in which these substances are stored—such, for instance, as the cell-walls in plants.

Digestion in the Mouth

And now let us take a mouthful of food and see how it is broken up, or **digested**, and how the nourishment in it is absorbed during its progress through the food-pipe.

We will take, as we often do, a piece of bread and a piece of meat together. Our piece of meat has a little fat upon it and thus the mouthful contains something of each of the three chief solid sorts of food-stuff: protein, fat, and starch.

We put the mouthful, then, into the mouth; and here we tear it and crush it with our teeth, and turn it and press it with the tongue.

In the course of our lives we have, as you know, two sets of teeth—the temporary or "milk-teeth," twenty in number, and the permanent teeth, thirty-two in number. The permanent teeth are of three kinds: in each jaw the four **incisors**, or cutters, in front; the two **canines** (from **canis**, a dog, because the dog has them so well developed), which are tearers, and are placed one on each side of the incisors; and the **molars**, or grinders, of which there are five on each side.

As we bite we feel a watery juice coming into our mouths, mingling with the food and making it all loose and soft, so that it is easy to swallow.

Whence does this "water" come? If you look at the diagram on page 22 you will see what look like three little pouches, which open into the mouth. These are not really pouches; each one consists of an innumerable host of tiny gland-cells, all crowded together, making a rather soft but solid lump.

Gland-cells and Glands

Now I must tell you that in their division of labour certain cells have taken upon themselves a most wonderful and important work—that of the making of juices. As fast as they draw in food and make it into protoplasm, so fast do they turn the protoplasm into a particular kind of juice. All do not make the same juice; and it usually happens that those which do make the same are clustered together, forming a mass which is called a **gland**, while the cells themselves are known as **gland-cells**. The business of making juice is called **secreting**; and the juices are often spoken of as **secretions**.

Ferments

Some of the juices secreted by glands contain a very marvellous substance called a **ferment**.

There are a number of ferments known to men of science, and they all have the power of producing some kind of change in particular substances when they are brought into contact with them. Some of these ferments are found, both in plants and in animals. We ourselves have ferments in our bodies. But as yet ferments are only known by what they **do**, some acting on one substance, some on another; no one yet knows exactly what they **are**.

The Salivary Glands

Well, the little pouches by the mouth are glands — called the **salivary glands**. Opening into the mouth by little pipes or **ducts**, they pour into it their juice, which is called **saliva**, and has a ferment in it. This ferment has no effect on the lean meat or the fat, which are not changed in the mouth except by being simply reduced to tiny pieces; but it has a great influence on the bread. The bread, as you know, is chiefly starch. Now starch is very difficult to make liquid—or to **dissolve**, as it is called. Without being dissolved it cannot be taken into the body. Hence it must first of all be somewhat altered; and it is the ferment in the saliva which brings about the necessary alteration. Wonderful to relate, it turns the starch into **sugar**. Sugar is a substance very closely related to starch, and, as you know, is quite easy to

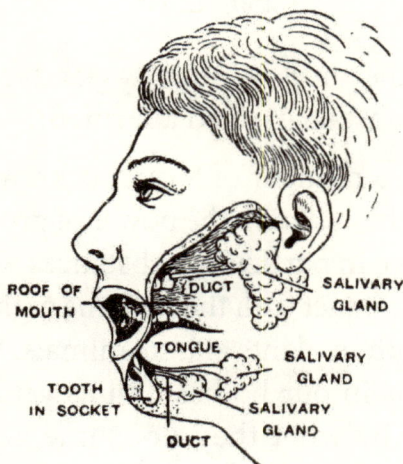

FIGURE 4 — THE SALIVARY GLANDS

dissolve. If you take a piece of stale bread by itself into your mouth, and bite it thoroughly, so that the saliva is well mixed up with it, you will detect the change that has taken place by finding that the bread tastes sweet.

This brings us to the reason why we should bite all our starchy foods well. We bite our meat in order to reduce it to small pieces; but we bite our bread, and our rice and potato, in order to mix the saliva in our mouths with the starch, and render it **soluble**—that is, easy to dissolve.

You will remember we found that the whole of the delicate skin of the food-pipe was lined with exceedingly small and fine blood-vessels. These are for ever taking up everything they can through their thin walls. As fast as food is dissolved it is thus passed into the blood. So when we have bitten up our mouthful of bread and meat, some of the starch of the bread, turned into sugar and quickly dissolved, has already passed into the blood by the tiny blood-vessels in the mouth.

The Gullet

All the rest of the food, the lean meat, the fat, and so much of the starch as has not yet been converted into sugar, is now rolled back over the tongue towards the throat. Then, by a push from the tongue and the muscles of the throat, it is sent down the straight part of the food-pipe called the **gullet**, or **esophagus**. After the food has passed down the throat we are not, in an ordinary way, aware of its passage through our body until it is near the end of the journey.

But you must not suppose that it just slips down, as water runs through a pipe. The walls of the gullet are made of muscle. This muscle contracts around and behind the food as it goes down, and so forces it on its way. Get a length of india-rubber tubing, and slip into the end of it a ball, about the same size round as the interior of the pipe. If you give a squeeze to the top part of the tubing, so as to force the ball down a little way, and go on squeezing thus, hand under hand, just over and behind the ball, till it comes out at the other end of your bit of pipe, you will get a rough idea of the way in which the muscles of the gullet act in pushing the food downwards into the stomach. If we swallow large, unwieldy pieces of food, we give the gullet hard work to get them down.

Digestion in the Stomach

Well, when our mouthful has passed the gullet and arrived at the stomach, it finds itself, as you may see by Figure 5 (p. 25), in a good-sized bag. This bag is lined with glands set closely side by side and opening into it. They secrete a juice called the **stomach**, or **gastric**, **juice**, which contains a ferment. Immediately on the arrival of the food, these glands begin pouring out their juice upon it. Now the ferment of the gastric juice has the particular power of dissolving proteins, so that it is here that the meat is digested. But the stomach is not only the place where proteins are dissolved, it is also the place where food of all sorts is churned until it is reduced to a kind of thick yellowish-grey cream, which is termed **chyme**.

This churning is done by the muscles of the wall of the stomach. I could not attempt to describe them to you here, but you should know that there are hardly any muscles in our whole body more wonderful than these. All the time the food is in the stomach, they are contracting and expanding—contracting and expanding —and thus hurling the food from one part of the stomach to another. This is fairly hard work, and you will readily understand that we make it much harder, and greatly fatigue the stomach, by sending down into it unsuitable or ill-bitten food.

The stomach goes on churning until the whole of the food is turned into **chyme**; there must not be any lumpy bits left. For if you look at Figure 5 again, you will see, marked at the lower end of the stomach, the

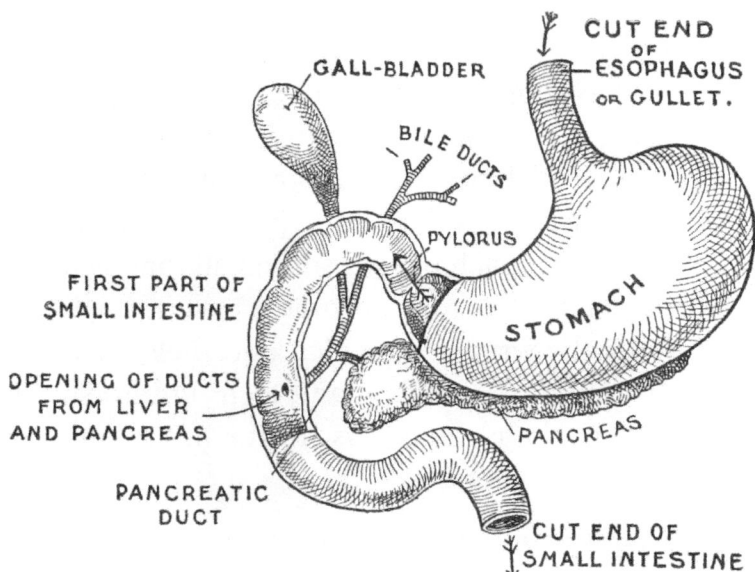

FIGURE 5 — DIAGRAM SHOWING HOW THE JUICES
OF THE LIVER AND PANCREAS ENTER THE INTESTINE

pylorus. Pylorus is a Greek word, and means "Keeper of the gate," and this name has been given to a strong ring of muscle which the food has to pass through before it can get out of the stomach into the first part of the small intestine. This keeper of the gate will let nothing big or rough go past him; he allows only a narrow opening, just enough for a small stream of thickish liquid to slip through. It is true that sometimes little hard things, such as pips and fruit-stones, manage to creep past, but this is an exceptional event, and only made possible by all the rest of the food being rendered so smooth and creamy that it helps them to glide through along with itself.

So that after our bread and meat have been for some time in the stomach—(it will take about three and a-half hours to digest them)—we should be very much puzzled to find them again.

What has happened? The proteins, or curdy part, of the lean meat, and the small quantity of protein which was in the bread, have been to a great extent dissolved out by the ferment in the gastric juice; the tiny blood-vessels of the stomach have absorbed all that has been dissolved, and it has now become a part of the blood itself. Only the wrappings which once held them are left in the stomach, crushed and torn up into shreds, not visible in the general mass of the liquid pulp. So much for the proteins.

The fat is still there, though we cannot distinguish it with our eyes; and so is the starch of the bread—so much of it as was not dissolved out in the mouth.

Action of Juices of the Liver, Pancreas, and Intestine

And now the chyme, being ready at last, slips through the pylorus, and, pushed on by the contracting muscles, finds itself in the small intestine.

If you look once more at Figure 5 you will see that it has arrived at the mouth of two ducts opening together into the small intestine from two bodies, which are drawn one on either side of the pipe.

These, again, as you may have guessed, are glands. The first, the largest gland in the body, is the **liver** (*see* the frontispiece), which lies for the most part at the back of the food-pipe, somewhat to the right. The juice which it secretes is called **bile** or **gall**; it does not contain a ferment. The liver is constantly at work making bile, and stores it ready for use in a little bag which you see marked on Figure 5 as the **gall-bladder**.

The second gland is the **pancreas** (*see* Figure 5 again). The juice from this gland is called the **pancreatic juice**. It contains three very powerful ferments.

No sooner has the food touched the mouth of the ducts than these two glands pour out their juices into it. A very important work of the bile is its action upon the fats in the food. Containing no ferment, it does not dissolve them, but it divides up the minute particles of fat into particles still more minute. In this it is assisted by the pancreatic juice, which, however, does a great deal besides. Helped by a ferment in the juices secreted by the intestine, it mingles with all the starchy food which has not been dissolved by the saliva in the mouth, and dissolves it. It also mingles with any proteins that may possibly have escaped the gastric juice in the stomach, and dissolves them too. In fact, the ferments in the pancreatic and intestinal juices are the most powerful of all the ferments in the food-pipe, and finish up the main part of digestion. After the bile and these juices have acted upon the food, it becomes more liquid and milky in appearance, and is then called **chyle**.

Meanwhile the food is being forced steadily onward along the small intestine. There must be no stopping anywhere, for as fast as the ferments work the food that is done with must be moved out of the way to make room for more.

What the Villi Do

Now, if you could see a piece of the inner coating of the small intestine, you would notice that it is more velvety in its appearance than the rest of the lining of the food-pipe; and if you examined it under the microscope, you would see that this velvety appearance is caused by an immense number of exceedingly minute projections. They cover the whole of the small intestine, more especially towards the upper end; and there are about five millions of them in all. These are called **villi**—from a Latin word **villus**, meaning a **tuft**—because they make the surface of the small intestine look rather shaggy compared with the rest of the food-pipe.

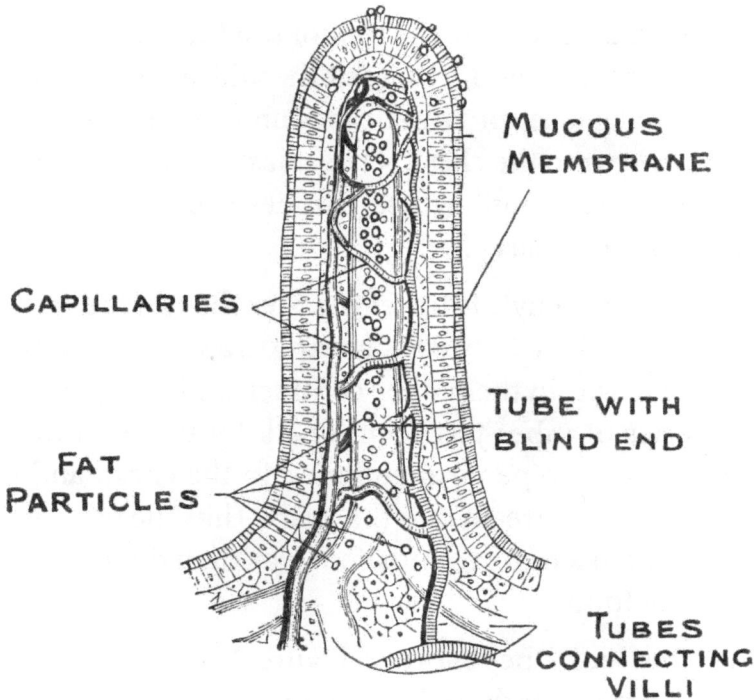

MUCOUS
MEMBRANE

CAPILLARIES

TUBE WITH
BLIND END

FAT
PARTICLES

TUBES
CONNECTING
VILLI

FIGURE 6 — A VILLUS, HIGHLY MAGNIFIED

A very good way to make yourself understand the difference between a gland in the intestine and a villus is to take a glove and draw it on to your hand, then turn it inside out, and draw your hand away, so that the fingers are left looking like holes with a pocket in each. These represent the glands opening into the intestine. Now turn your glove back ready for putting on again; the fingers will then represent the villi, as they hang with their blind or closed ends into the food-pipe. Only you will not forget that the villi and the glands are very, very small.

Each villus has inside it a cage-like network of the most minute blood-vessels, within which again is a little tube with a blind end. The millions of these little tubes, joining together at the bases of the villi, are connected up to make a set of larger tubes and these, gradually passing up into the chest, form at last a pipe, about the size of a goose-quill, which empties itself into a large vein near the heart.

When the chyle is travelling over the villi they suck up from it all the fatty part. Having drawn this into the little tube within them, they contract, and pump it into the series of tubes just mentioned. By these, in time, it reaches the pipe we mentioned in the chest, and is poured in one stream into the heart. Thus the fats enter the blood in a more roundabout way than do the other forms of food.

Now look once more at Figure 3 (page 17), and observe the length and the many coils of the small intestine. In such a length of food-pipe, with tiny blood-vessels all over every part of it, eager to absorb into the blood whatever food has been dissolved by the processes of digestion, it is clear that but little of what is useful to the body can be lost.

But as the food passes on in this way, parting with its substance to the blood, it must necessarily diminish in bulk; and the more nourishment there is in it, the more it will thus be reduced. At first sight this might seem to be an advantage, but if we look closer at the matter, we shall see that the food being so much less in bulk makes a difficulty for the food-pipe. The food can only move by means of that continual contraction of the muscle which we illustrated with the india-rubber pipe a little while ago. It is more difficult to force the food along the coils of the intestine, which have so many turnings and twistings, and lie more or less horizontally, than it is to force it down a straight vertical tube like the gullet. And the difficulty is much greater if the mass to be pushed along is a small one; for then the muscles have nothing to close over, nothing to give a good squeeze to; they can only more or less press upon themselves. It is here that such food-stuffs as fruit and vegetables are very useful. They contain but little nourishment, and none of the juices or ferments of the food-pipe can dissolve much out of them except water and the salts I told you of. They are thus sent along practically unchanged, forming a mass for the muscles to push upon, and making easier the general movement of the food. It is of the utmost importance that, the food in the intestine should be kept steadily though slowly, moving; a stoppage in its movement may indeed become actually dangerous to life; hence we see that it is important to eat a certain amount of fruit or green vegetables with our food.

Food in the Large Intestine

When the food has passed from the small into the large intestine it has become nearly all solid—for as fast as that part of it which is useful to the body was dissolved out of it, the tiny blood-vessels absorbed it into the blood. Now only shreds and remains of useless matter are left.

If you look at Figure 3 again, you will see that the place where the small intestine widens into the large intestine makes rather a sharp corner, and that a little finger-like projection is drawn coming down from that part. This little projection is called the **vermiform** (or wormlike) **appendix**; and it has an opening into the intestine. It is important to notice it, because sometimes pips, or fruitstones, or bits of nuts, which have not been digested, lodge in this opening as they pass by it, or get right into the vermiform appendix, and cause it to become inflamed. This inflammation is a serious illness, which you may have heard spoken of as "appendicitis." It may, indeed, be due to other causes besides the one mentioned here still, we should remember that it is unwise to swallow fruitstones and pips.

In the Rectum

From the larger intestine the food passes into the **rectum** (Figure 3); and, when it is there, we once more become aware of it: we are warned, as it were, that there is rubbish waiting to be cast out of us for if it stays with us any longer it will do us harm.

The rubbish is then cast out through the **anus**, the opening at the lower end of the food-pipe and so we come to the end of the journey of the food through our bodies, and of the history of its transformation by the way.

How it is all Done

And now I think there must be many thoughtful readers who have been wondering how this is all accomplished. What makes the muscles contract? What makes the glands secrete? What causes the juices from the glands to gush forth? How, too, is our tongue able to taste? and how is that message conveyed to us which tells us to cast out the rubbish from the food-pipe?

Both the movements which we are aware of, and the movements we are not aware of, are set up and governed by the brain and nervous system. Nerve-threads run to the brain from every part of the food-pipe, and back again to every part of it from the brain. When food is placed in our mouths, the first set of nerves convey the news to the brain, and instantly, along the second set, is sped the command to bite it and prepare to swallow it. Every movement made, as well as the pouring out of the saliva and the tasting of the tongue—all is caused and controlled by the action of the brain and nerves.

But you will ask me how it is that we know what is happening in the mouth, and to some extent what is happening in the rectum, but do not know what is going on in the rest of the food-pipe.

That is because, as we shall see more fully in another place, there are two great divisions of the brain; one of these is, as it were, the home of all our knowledge and of our will, and we are aware of the messages which it receives, and of the movements which it causes. But the other part of the brain works for us without our being aware of what it does. The nerves of the mouth, and some of the nerves of the rectum, run up to the first division of the brain; and so we know what is happening in these two parts of the food-pipe, and we have power over them. But the nerves from the rest of the food-pipe go to the other part of the brain, and thus all the long and manifold work of digesting our food is performed without our consciousness.

Is not this a very wonderful thing?—and also of very great advantage to us? Think what it would be if we were obliged, as the saying is, to give our minds to digesting our food. It would take up so much of our attention that we should have none left for anything else. Now we eat our meals, and get up from the table, and go off to our work or our play and while we are busy with these, and have quite forgotten our food in the food-pipe, it is being digested for us, absorbed into our blood, and built up into our bodies, without our having any trouble about it.

Yet we must never forget that if it were not for the brain and the nerves this work of the food-pipe could not be done.

Importance of Taking Care of the Body

Now, all wise men and women are diligent about taking care of the body for if people do not take care of their bodies they become weak and sickly, and perhaps downright ill.

From what you have now learnt of the food-pipe I am sure you can see what an important part of the body it is, and therefore how important it is to treat it well.

Let us go shortly through the main things to be remembered in our care of it.

Care of the Teeth

In the first place, as we have already seen, we ought not to swallow our food in big lumps; and, to avoid this we must make good use of our teeth. We must bite our food up small, and not forget that bread and other starchy foods are to be partly digested in the mouth by mixing them well with saliva. Now, this is a matter of habit. Every sensible boy and girl will take pains to get into the habit of biting food thoroughly, knowing well what is the harm done by "bolting" it.

But to bite well we must have good teeth and in order to have good teeth we must spend some trouble upon them. You know that the surface of our teeth is covered with a whitish substance called **enamel**. This enamel is exceedingly hard—in fact, it is the hardest part of the tooth. Within it is a layer of bone-like matter called **dentine**, considerably softer than the enamel and within the dentine, again, is a cavity or hole, in which is a still softer **pulp**. If the enamel is worn away the softer parts of the tooth must be exposed and on being exposed they decay. Once gone, the enamel can never be replaced so do not damage it by cracking nuts.

What is it that may destroy the enamel of our teeth

and cause the dentine to decay? I must tell you more fully about this later on; here I will only say that any substance from the food we eat, when left upon the teeth, begins to decay and this decay attacks the enamel too, and, as we say, eats it away. It is especially bad for the teeth to have little bits of food sticking between them.

To prevent the destruction of the enamel we must keep our teeth clean. We should brush them thoroughly with fresh water and a little tooth-powder, at least twice a day, on getting up in the morning and going to bed at night. We must be careful about the choice of a tooth-powder, for many of the pastes and powders advertised are very injurious to the enamel; in fact, it is better to use nothing but water and the tooth-brush than to use them. A good powder which will help cleanse the teeth and do no harm to the enamel is camphorated or plain powdered chalk. After applying the chalk a little common yellow soap may be used. The chalk can be obtained from ground oyster shells.

Some people will tell you that the milk-teeth of children need not be brushed; but this is a very serious mistake. For if the milk-teeth decay, they infect the permanent teeth which lie close beside them in the gums waiting to come through and the permanent teeth, once injured in this way, can never be cured.

When brushing one's teeth it is a good thing, at the same time, to rinse the mouth out and gargle the throat. For this last purpose, you should dissolve in water two or three crystals of "permanganate of potash." For one penny you can buy enough of it to last you six months and it will cleanse the mouth and throat very effectually. People do not always pay sufficient attention to keeping the mouth as a whole clean; yet it is an exceedingly important part of the food-pipe, for anything harmful collecting there may be swallowed down, and may then be passed into the body.

Care of the Tongue

In another way we ought also to take care of the tongue. The tongue is the seat, or as we call it, the **organ**, of the sense of taste; and this sense, if we do not spoil it, is exceedingly useful to us in judging of our food. In fact, it is for this reason that it is placed at the beginning of the food-pipe, so that, if the nerves of the tongue send to the brain the message, Here is something nasty, the brain may send back the order, Do not swallow it; and so we can put it out of our mouths. Of course when we are ill, we sometimes have to take nasty medicine but that is exceptional. If our bodies are healthy, and the food-pipe and the nerves working as they are meant to do, then our tongue will tell us truly what is good for us and what is not. Thus you may have been eating an apple, biting pieces from it without looking, and so have taken into your mouth a part which was brown and rotten. Did not your tongue instantly tell you that that part was nasty and bitter—not fit to be swallowed; and did not you instantly prevent yourself from swallowing it?

I think the tongue might be called "gate-keeper" as well as the pylorus muscle—do not you? It has to keep the gate of the throat, as the pylorus keeps the gate of the small intestine.

How to Spoil One's Sense of Taste

Unfortunately a great many people spoil their sense of taste, so that it is of little use to them. This is a serious matter, for they are thus led to eat and drink many harmful things. Our sense of taste, if properly educated, likes plain and simple food for the most part—bread, fruit, milk, meat, sugar, and so on. But we often force it to accept foods that are highly seasoned, having different strong-tasting substances mixed with them. The nerves of taste, after rebelling for a little while, get used, as we say, to these new things—even grow to be pleased with them; and then their messages to the brain no longer tell whether the food is good or not. Once accustomed to highly-seasoned food, the tongue can hardly taste the simple, wholesome things which before seemed pleasant.

One of the substances with which people spoil their sense of taste is strong, over-drawn tea. Another, yet more injurious, is alcohol. When we first take it our tongue gives us faithful warning: This is not good; this must be spat out. I do not think a single person tasting beer, wine, or spirits for the first time ever thinks them pleasant to drink. He probably makes quite a fearful grimace because they taste so disagreeable. But many persons, as we know, neglect that faithful warning. They force the tongue into a habit of liking alcohol, and by doing so they make the tongue incapable of tasting aright. Yet another substance which spoils the taste is tobacco. No one whose tongue is being constantly exposed to the juice or the fumes of tobacco can taste properly, as he was meant to do.

So in order to keep our sense of taste healthful, we must eat good and plainly prepared food, and we must not use either strong tea, alcohol, or tobacco.

But perhaps you will say it does not matter so much about the tongue, provided the rest of the food-pipe gets on all right. Yes, but the rest of the food-pipe gets on very badly if you have a poor gate-keeper, who lets things through anyhow. Some of the foods which you may have grown to think pleasant give the stomach a great deal of trouble, and perhaps, after all, supply very little nourishment. Others are actually hurtful, some in one way and some in another; whilst the alcohol, which is not a food at all, and is of no use to a person in ordinary health, interferes with the work of digestion, and does serious harm in several ways. We shall see this later on when we come to consider what we should take and what we should avoid in eating and drinking.

Getting Rid of Waste Matter

Another point I must mention about the care of the food-pipe is the necessity for getting rid of the rubbish regularly. What would you think of a person who should collect into a bag all the old cabbage stalks, potato skins, scraps of gristle, and bones remaining from his meals, and should carry this bagful constantly about with him—at table, in bed, going about his business—everywhere. You would say he was a mad person, and his ways disgusting, and you would be quite right. And yet we are sometimes apt, through carelessness, to act in the very same manner, and carry about with us rubbish which ought to be quickly got rid of.

If the waste matter from our food is allowed to collect day by day in the large intestine, it greatly hinders the working of the food-pipe. Moreover, it soon begins to decompose, that is, to break up into different separate substances, and some of it then passes into the blood, where it acts as a poison. Then one begins to feel heavy and uncomfortable, depressed and unable to enjoy either work or play; very likely one has a bad headache, and still more likely one is very cross. If this state of things continues, a number of troublesome ailments may be started, and the person who has not troubled to take care of his food-pipe in this particular respect, may be all his life hampered and weakened.

The lower part of the food-pipe should, as a rule, be emptied once every day and the best time for attending to this matter is in the morning, soon after breakfast. This is very much a question of habit; we can train our food-pipe to be ready to cast out the rubbish at a fixed time every day, just as by constant neglect we can get it into the very bad habit of keeping the rubbish in for a great length of time. At no time of life can a good habit be formed so well as in quite early childhood, and I should advise any of my girl readers who have the care of baby brothers and sisters to take thought to help them with regard to this. Animals here set us a very good example; any boy who has a dog knows how regular he is in taking a run for the purpose of attending to this need of his body.

There are three ways in which we can make the getting rid of the rubbish easy. First, as we have seen, by forming a good habit and not neglecting the warning given us by the nerves of the rectum. Secondly, by taking a proper amount of exercise—for if we sit still a great deal the muscles of the food-pipe are apt to get sluggish. And thirdly, by eating a sufficient quantity of vegetables and fruit, which, as we saw, are a help to the muscles of the intestine in squeezing the food along. Baked apples and the use of salad oil with our vegetables are particularly good for this purpose.

It is a very great mistake to be often taking medicines to help us; for, by doing so, we weaken the action of the muscles, and accustom them to rely on outside assistance, instead of playing their own part, as they were meant to do.

Tight Clothing to be Avoided

There is just one more thing to say here about the care of the food-pipe. It ought never, in any part of it, to be compressed or squeezed together. Such squeezing hinders the action of the glands and muscles and also the flow of blood through the tiny blood-vessels which absorb the food. Hence no sensible person will wear tight clothes—all clothing should be loose. The stomach, the liver, and the pancreas are situated, as you may see in the diagrams, about the region of the waist, and so are very apt to be injured by stays and tight belts. I need hardly tell you that such injuries may become grave and even when that is not the case, a weakening of these very important organs must mean a weakening of the whole body.

CHAPTER III

RESPIRATION

"With every breath I sigh myself away,
And take my tribute from the wandering wind,
To fan the flame of life's consuming fire."

— OLIVER WENDELL HOLMES

WHEN, in days very, very long ago, men first began to think about themselves, and to know that they were alive, they discovered that all creatures which are alive breathe, and that when they cease to breathe they die.

And as these ancient people pondered over this, they saw that a dead man, a man who had ceased to breathe, was not only motionless, unable to fight or hunt any more, but was also without thought and without sense.

It was therefore only natural that they should believe that breath and life and the power of thought were all one and the same thing; and thus it happens that in most languages many of the words used to express life and thought originally meant simply **breath**.

Did the men of those early times judge rightly? Now that we know so much more than they did about living things, can we still say, "The breath is the life," or, "The breath is the thought"?

Yes; for all the ordinary purposes of life and action, we must still say so. Without breathing we cannot move, speak, or think—we are dead, or as if we were dead.

What Breathing Means

By breathing we mean drawing into our bodies some of the air around us, and then expelling it again. All our lives long we are inhaling, or breathing in, and then exhaling, or breathing out. Of what use to us is the air we breathe? Why could we not live without it? Let us consider this.

You know that the air does not consist of one gas by itself, but principally of two gases mingled in a certain proportion. Of these the one which is known as **oxygen** forms about a fifth part of the atmosphere. Now this oxygen is most wonderfully ready to unite with other substances. At a certain degree of heat the free oxygen in the air will unite with the **carbon**, which forms a part of all vegetable and animal substance and this process of uniting we call **burning**. The oxygen and the carbon, as they seize upon one another, break down the substance—the wood, or coal, or fat—which contained the carbon, and destroy it, leaving in the end only a heap of ashes. Meanwhile the air all around becomes very hot, and, in most cases, we have flashes of light, more or less steady, which we call **flames**.

Let us take a bit of candle and light it, and let us, for one moment, watch it burning and think over what is happening. That candle contains carbon both in the fat of which it is made and in the wick; it only requires a certain degree of heat to enable it to seize upon the oxygen of the air. You gave it that heat by putting your lighted match to the wick, and now the seizing of oxygen is going on merrily, and we who stand by perceive it as light, and also as heat. There is plenty of oxygen in the air of the room, and, if we allow it to do so, this seizing of oxygen—this **burning**—will go on until all the carbon is used up, and the candle is, as we say, burnt out.

And what has become of the carbon and oxygen which were united together in the burning? They have formed an invisible gas, called **carbon dioxide**, which can stop the burning and extinguish the flame when there is not enough free oxygen present to prevent it.

Let us get a tall glass jar, quite dry inside, and put it over the burning candle. You know what follows: the candle goes out. If you reflect you will know why this happens: because the oxygen in the enclosed air has united with the carbon of the candle to form the invisible gas, carbon dioxide, which has stifled the flame.

Notice, too, that the inside of the jar has become misty with moisture. This shows us that water was in the candle, and that it has been set free by the burning.

In this instance of the burning candle we get a bright, steady flame. Nevertheless, we must bear in mind that in itself burning does not consist in the production of a flame. In itself burning is simply the union of oxygen with another substance —mostly, in our everyday experience, with carbon.

As we shall see in a moment, this may take place somewhat more slowly than in the burning candle, and produce no light or glow. On the other hand, it cannot take place without producing **heat**—greater or less in degree, according to the rapidity of the burning.

Let us now go back to ourselves and see what happens when we breathe.

The oxygen in the air passes into our blood, and is carried by the blood-stream to every part of our bodies.

As it travels in and out through all the tissues, the oxygen unites with the carbon from them and thus forms carbon dioxide. This carbon dioxide then passes into the blood in exchange for the oxygen.

But this is burning, you will say; it is the same thing as we saw happening in the case of the burning candle!

You are right; this is burning, though, of course, it is a burning without flame. This burning is our life. It is this which gives us heat, and heat gives us energy—not only the energy which enables us to run, or to shout, or to work hard, but also the energy which keeps our heart beating, which makes the food-pipe digest food, and enables the brain to think and to control the whole body.

When this heat is withdrawn the brain loses its power to govern; then the heart stops beating, and all the muscles cease to work. If within a very short time the power to breathe is not restored, life, as we often say, becomes extinct; the burning goes quite out and cannot be kindled again.

This is why we may truly say, "The breath is the life."

All animals and plants breathe, as we know; but the burning is not equally rapid in them all, and hence the heat and energy are not equally great in all.

The rapidity and the heat of the burning depend, however, not only on the breathing itself, but also, as we shall see in the next chapter, on the rapidity with which the blood carrying the oxygen is sent round all the body.

You will find it very interesting work to try and discover for yourselves which animals are the hottest and most energetic, and which are most cold and slow.

The Breathing Organs

Let us see first what organs or apparatus we have to breathe with, and then consider how these work.

The best plan, in order to understand this, is to get the lungs and windpipe of a sheep and examine them. If you cannot do so, look carefully at the accompanying diagrams (Figures 7 and 8).

You will see that in front of the gullet we have another pipe, also opening into the mouth, which runs down as far as the upper part of the chest, where it branches into two. Each of these two branches again divides into two, and these into two again and this branching goes on until we have at last pipes of such excessive fineness that they cannot be distinguished by the naked eye. All these together form two large masses, each depending from one of the original branches of the pipe. I daresay you already know that the pipe is

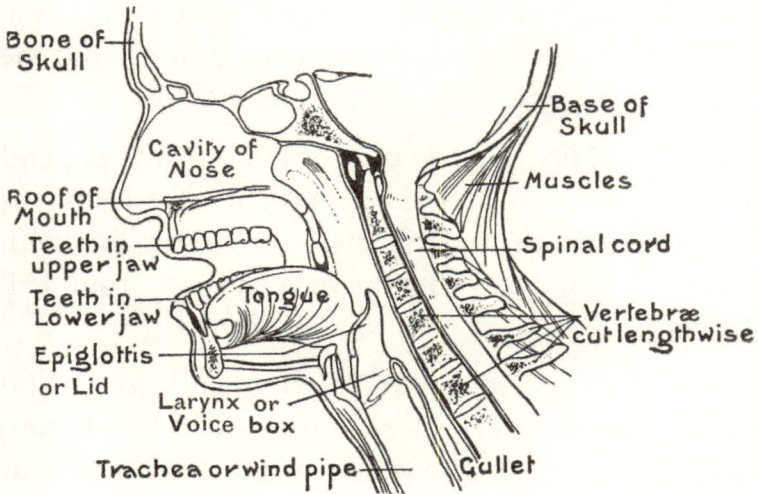

FIGURE 7 — HEAD AND NECK,
CUT THROUGH LENGTHWISE

called the **windpipe**; that the two branches are the **bronchi**; and that the masses, or lobes, composed of the fine tubes are the **lungs**.

If you compare the windpipe with the gullet of a sheep, you will see that while the latter is soft and will fall together, the windpipe is held open by rings of cartilage. Notice, though, that the rings are not entire: there is a gap at the back where the gullet adjoins the windpipe. Can you tell me the reason of this?—If the stiff cartilage went the whole way round, it would hinder the muscles of the gullet from pushing down the food, and we could hardly swallow.

Cartilage holds open the bronchi also, and goes a considerable distance down into the branching tubes ending only when they are reduced very much in size.

WIND PIPE
OR TRACHEA

RINGS OF
CARTILAGE

BRONCHUS

AIR PIPES

AIR SACS

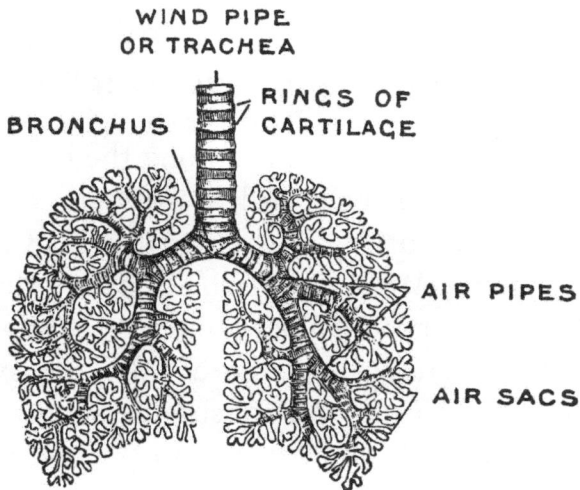

FIGURE 8 — THE WINDPIPE AND LUNGS

I need hardly tell you that the tubes are held open in this manner in order to let the air pass through them quickly and without hindrance.

You will notice that the widest part of the windpipe is at the top, and if you could look into this part you would see two ridges, one on either side. This is the **voice-box** or, if you like the scientific name, the **larynx** and these ridges are what are known as the **vocal cords.** It is the vibration of these vocal cords, worked by very wonderful muscles, which makes the voice. Their action is too intricate for me to describe it to you here; indeed, you have only to think of the many different notes and tones to which a person can give utterance, and you will understand that the mechanism of the voice-box must be a complicated one.

Gentle Voice and Quiet Speech

A beautiful voice is among the best of gifts; and a voice that is beautiful in ordinary speech is even more to be prized than one which is beautiful only in singing. Whether we shall possess this gift or no depends very much upon ourselves and on the pains we take to cultivate it and to avoid what may be harmful. Rough shouting and constant loud talking are very injurious, especially to a young voice; they make it harsh, disagreeable and weak, so that in time it becomes very uncomfortable to its owner and jars on the ears of those who hear it. We should practise speaking gently and clearly, using the lips freely to frame our words. Such speaking is far better heard than mere loud noise. It exercises the muscles concerned in the right way, and gives them more and more ease and delicacy of action, so that the voice becomes sweeter and clearer the more it is used.

How the Windpipe is Protected

We have seen that the windpipe opens into the mouth as the gullet does. Suppose some food should go down the windpipe by mistake. This does happen, though very rarely, if we are swallowing carelessly, or perhaps talking, laughing, and eating at the same time. Then, if a piece of food goes down the wrong way, as we call it, we choke and gasp, and cough, suffering very great discomfort, until at last we get it up again and the windpipe is freed. If it cannot be got back again the consequences may be most serious; as you know, people may die by being choked in this way.

But this need hardly happen, for nature has provided us with the means of closing the windpipe when in the act of swallowing. At the opening of it, and just behind the tongue, you may see a gristly projection, which forms a little lid. As the tongue moves backward to send the food into the gullet, it presses the little gristly lid, the **epiglottis**, down upon the top of the windpipe, and so removes any danger of the food slipping into it by mistake.

How the Fresh Air Reaches the Blood

When we breathe, the muscles which form the floor and walls of the chest expand and partly because the lungs are attached to them by wrappings of tissue, they are forced to expand too. Into the open space thus made the air rushes, passing through the nostrils, down the wide open windpipe and bronchi, and into all those innumerable and tiny pipes which form the mass of the lungs.

And then what becomes of it?

Each of those minute pipes ends in an equally minute sac (Figure 8), the membrane of which is thin and delicate enough to allow of a fluid substance passing through it. Round each of these sacs is wrapped a network of the minutest blood-vessels, whose walls are equally delicate. These blood-vessels are charged with carbon dioxide produced by the burning which goes on in the body, and in the lungs this carbon dioxide passes out of the blood, while the pure air with its oxygen passes in to take its place.

As the muscles of the chest-wall and the floor of the chest contract again, they compress or squeeze the lungs together, and so force out the carbon dioxide, which otherwise would poison the body.

With the carbon dioxide are exhaled water-vapour and also numbers of cells, which have died off at the surface of the mucous membrane, just as we shall find the upper layer of cells dies off on the surface of the outer skin.

It would be very harmful if these substances were allowed to accumulate in the sacs and tubes of the lungs and we find a most wonderful arrangement for preventing this. A large number of cells on the inner surface of the windpipe, the bronchi, and the bigger tubes have lengthened themselves out into tiny whips, making together a kind of fringe. These move unceasingly, always in one direction, upwards towards the mouth and nostrils. This produces a sort of sweeping movement which forces water, dust particles, loose cells, anything in the way of rubbish which may have got into the tubes, up and out through the nostrils or the mouth. If it were not for the activity of these lash-like or **ciliated cells**, as they are called, many people, such as miners, or those who work in mills, would often be nearly suffocated by the dust which they breathe into their lungs.

And now, perhaps, someone may say to me, "It is all very well to tell us that water and carbon dioxide and cells come out of our mouths when we breathe out, but we do not see anything of the kind when we breathe." Well, on a cold day you may see the water-vapour in your breath condensing into mist and forming a little cloud in front of your face while if you breathe on a very cold window-pane or piece of metal, you may see the moisture condense yet further, and trickle down in drops. So it is plain that we breathe out water.

You can see for yourselves by a little experiment that we breathe out carbon dioxide. Get a small quantity of fresh, clear lime-water, and pour it into a tumbler or shallow glass jar. Blow your breath right down into it through a straw. The lime-water looks perfectly clear, yet it contains a substance—lime—which is always ready to unite with carbon dioxide. When the two are united, they form a white powdery substance, chalk, easily seen in the water. As you breathe down your straw, you will see the water growing milkier and milkier in appearance. It is full of carbon dioxide combined with lime, and the carbon dioxide has been supplied by your breath.

If you have a friend or teacher who is interested in chemistry, you should ask him or her to show you an experiment which proves that the jar in which our candle burnt out is also full of this same gas, and that it contained scarcely any before the candle was burnt in it.

As for the cells, you must take my word for them at present; but I may tell you that a clever experimenter has contrived to catch them on carefully prepared moist surfaces at a distance of many feet in front of the person who breathed them out.

Importance of Plenty of Fresh Air

If, as we said just now, the breath is the life, I am sure you will agree with me when I say that every sensible person will take the greatest care as to all that is connected with breathing.

Let me tell you one or two things that should be borne in mind.

First, you will remember, what I have mentioned already, that it is the brain which governs all the work of our bodies, whether it be work we are aware of, or work, like that of digestion for instance, of which we are not aware. Of all the parts of the body, none requires so much oxygen as the brain. If the brain has plenty of oxygen, so that the fire within it burns strongly, then our thoughts are quick and clear, our movements well governed, and the different organs of the body play their part as they were meant to do. But if the fire within the brain burns low and weak, then we become gloomy and drowsy, what we do is apt to be badly done, and all the organs of the body act more slowly and feebly than they should. We very often see people who, without being actually ill, and without having any particular trouble, are constantly cross and miserable. In very many cases their discomfort is caused by their not having breathed in enough oxygen, so that the fire within them is not strong enough and the brain is left dull.

Well, to prevent such a state of things as this, and to keep the brain and the whole body active and vigorous and happy, we must have plenty of good fresh air. We must be out of doors as much as we can, and when we are obliged to be indoors we must throw our windows open and let in the air from outside. For a person, as he breathes, uses up oxygen very fast, and casts out, as you saw, carbon dioxide, water, and used-up cells from his lungs and mouth, and it is simply taking in poison to breathe this all in again. In a later chapter we shall see how to manage a building so as to secure sufficient fresh air for the persons within it; here I will only repeat again: Take pains to have as much fresh air as you can; remember that health, vigour, happiness, success depend greatly on this.

The Right Way to Breathe

But a person may be upon a glorious moor, or out on the open sea, surrounded by the purest and freshest air in the world, and if he does not breathe it in properly he will get very little good from it.

Can you tell me how one must breathe to breathe properly?

First—Breathe through the nose. In the passages of the nose any particles of dust or other substances floating in the air are caught on hairs and on the mucous membrane, as well as on ciliated cells like those in the windpipe, which sweep them out into the air again. The air as it passes along is, moreover, rendered warm and somewhat moist, so that, when it reaches the windpipe and lungs, it does not irritate their delicate mucous membrane. If anyone who reads this book has any difficulty in breathing through the nose, he (or she) should mention it to his (or her) parents or teacher, who may then ask a doctor about it. The causes of such a difficulty can often be easily removed when one is young, and attention to this may make an immense difference to a person's health and strength during the whole of life. At the same time, you should remember that breathing properly is also a question of habit, and that many people breathe through their mouths simply because they do not take any pains to form the good habit of breathing through the nose.

Secondly—Breathe deep; draw the fresh air far down into the lung, and when you exhale, or breathe out, do so thoroughly, so as to get rid of as much carbon dioxide and rubbish as you can. Numbers of people draw the fresh air only a little way down into the lung, and expel the impure air only from the top part of it. Hence the air in the lower part, or base, of the lungs is very slowly changed; the body gets too little oxygen, and a great deal of carbon dioxide is retained in it. This is obviously not a good thing, and we should accustom ourselves to draw the air well down into the lungs. And here we come upon another kind of harm done by tight clothing. If the chest is not allowed to expand freely, and as far as it can go, we cannot breathe deep. Women and girls who tight-lace or wear a dress-bodice made tight over the chest, cannot possibly draw good breaths of air right down into the bases of the lungs, and therefore, whatever they may say to the contrary, we know that neither their brains nor the rest of their bodies can be as healthy and vigorous as they might be. The very form of the ribs is affected by tight lacing, as you may see from Figures 9 and 9A.

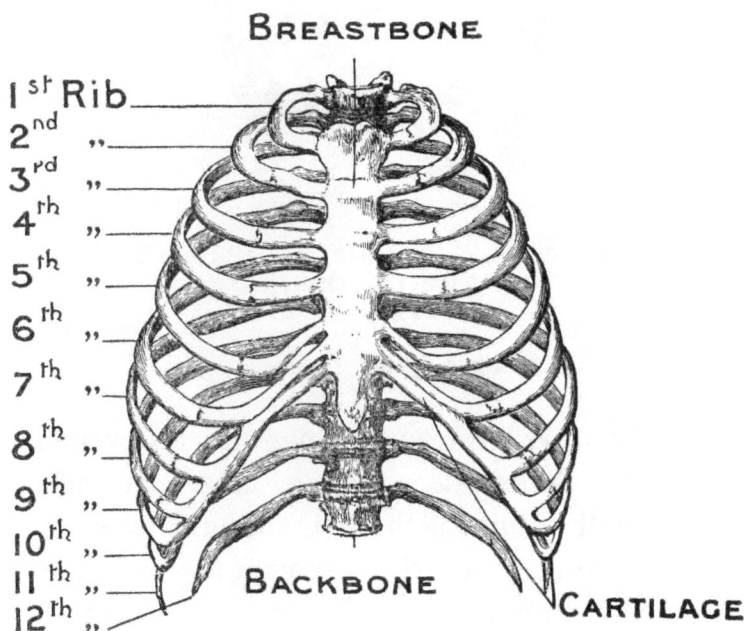

FIGURE 9 — NATURAL FORM OF THE RIBS

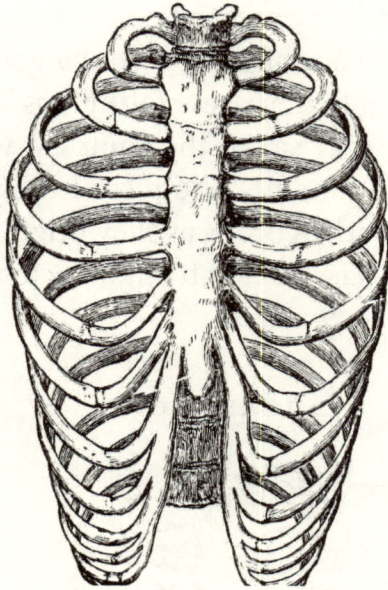

FIGURE 9A — THE RIBS COMPRESSED
BY TIGHT CLOTHING

Necessity for Exercise

But, however loose our clothing and however good
a habit of breathing deep we may have acquired, we
cannot rapidly change all the air in the lungs by ordinary
quiet breathing. To do this we must take exercise of
some vigorous kind, and as the point of such exercise is
to quickly fill the whole of the lungs with clean, fresh air,
you will readily understand that it ought to be taken out
of doors. As we run, or walk briskly, or row, without our
troubling about it, the fresh air passes into the depths
of the lungs and the stale air is expelled. That is why
after exercise—unless, indeed, we have over-fatigued
ourselves by using our muscles unwisely—we feel so
much brighter and are able to think so much more

quickly and clearly than before. Properly speaking, everyone who is in ordinary health ought to spend at least two hours in the day taking exercise in the open air. Those whose work makes this impossible should learn certain physical exercises—more particularly breathing exercises—and practise these vigorously for a certain time every day and if they cannot do this out of doors they should be careful to have their window wide open while they are exercising so as to get all the fresh air they can to draw into their lungs,

Alcohol Weakens the Tissue of Lungs

Now that you know what is meant by the saying, "The breath is the life," I am sure you will see what a sad thing it is that men should ever dull and weaken this fire within them by bad habits or carelessness.

One bad habit which has this effect is that of drinking alcohol. Little by little, alcohol weakens the tissues of the lungs; the delicate membranes through which the passage of the air takes place are spoilt; and if the mischief is not stopped the tissue of the lungs may be attacked by the germs of disease, like consumption, and in the end destroyed. As you know, destruction of all the lung-tissue means destruction of the whole body.

And now you have finished this chapter I hope you will spring up, throw open the window, and take some good deep breaths to get your brain ready for the next thing you have to do or, better still, have a run out of doors and fill your lungs with the freshness of the open air.

CHAPTER IV

THE CIRCULATION

"We recognise a grandeur in the beating of the heart."

— Wordsworth

The Story of William Harvey

On April 1st, 1578, there was born, at Folkestone, in Kent, William Harvey, the son of a well-to-do yeoman. His father was able to give him a good education; and after leaving school he went to Caius College, Cambridge. When the time came for him to choose his work in life, he decided to be a physician.

In those days the city of Padua, in Italy, was famous for its learning in anatomy. Anatomy is the name given to the science which treats of all the parts of the human body and their uses. In order that he might study under the greatest masters of this science, William Harvey went to Padua but though he took his degree of doctor of medicine, he was not satisfied with what he had learnt. He thought there were many things in the working of the human body which had not yet been thoroughly explained; more particularly, he was of opinion that no one had yet discovered the true nature of the heart, and the true reason for its beating, nor had found out how the flow of the blood was caused and directed.

On his return to England, in 1603, he set himself to find this out. He lived in London and practised as a physician, working also at St. Bartholomew's Hospital, and as a lecturer on anatomy and medicine. He soon became very well known; in fact, in 1618 he was appointed physician extraordinary to James I., and later on physician to Charles I.

No doubt his practice and the fame and wealth it brought him gave him pleasure, but his chief interest and his chief delight were in his search to find out why the heart beats and how the blood flows.

Until his time the great anatomists had examined for the most part only dead bodies, in which they could indeed see the position and shape of different organs, but could not tell how they worked. Harvey by no means neglected this method of observation; in fact, it is said that his skill in it, and the knowledge he gained by it, were greater than had ever been seen before; but he also introduced a new method of discovering the truth about the working of the body: he examined with great care, as far as he possibly could, the living bodies both of men and of animals.

It would take me too long to tell you about his experiments. In the course of them he worked at pigs, dogs, snakes, fishes, oysters, insects, and many other creatures. He was the first to find out how useful a knowledge of the anatomy of animals is to anyone who wishes to understand human anatomy.

For nineteen years Harvey worked at this puzzle of the heart-beat and the flow of the blood. He would not say he had found out the secret until, by great numbers of observations and experiments, he had made himself quite sure that he was right. But when he was lecturing to students he told them from time to time what researches he was making, and what were the results of them, so that a number of people, both in England and abroad, knew what he was working at, and followed his work with the greatest interest.

At last, in the year 1628, he published a short book, written in Latin, in which he set forth clearly what he had discovered, namely, how and why the heart beats, and what is the course of the blood through the body. This discovery is one of the greatest ever made; and perhaps we English people may be allowed to be proud that an Englishman made it.

What Harvey Discovered

And now—what was this discovery? It was this. The heart, which is formed of very strong and wonderful muscles, acts as a ceaselessly-working pump.

By alternately contracting and expanding it pumps the blood round and round the body; and since, as you know, the blood bears on its current both the food we eat and the air we breathe, it is by this means that the body is warmed and fed. The course of the blood is called the **circulation**.

The heart has two great divisions, one on the right,

the other on the left. They are separated by a wall of muscle so thick that no blood can pass through.

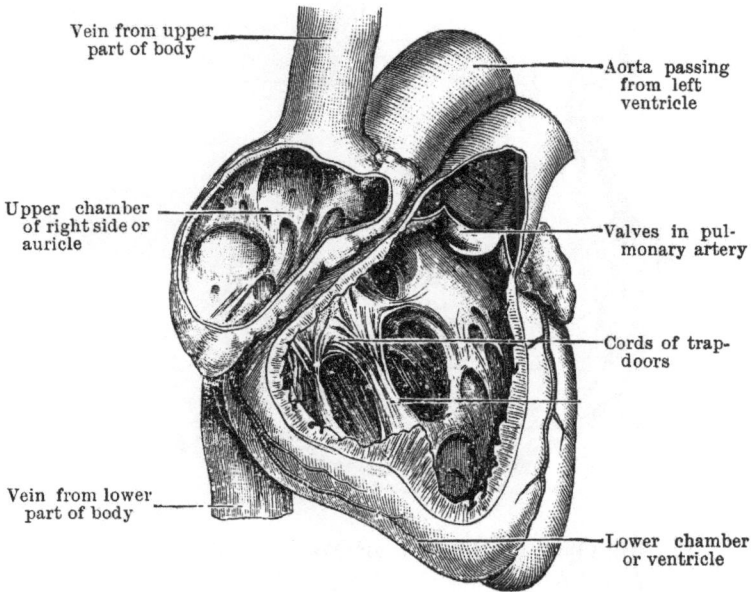

Vein from upper part of body

Aorta passing from left ventricle

Upper chamber of right side or auricle

Valves in pulmonary artery

Cords of trapdoors

Vein from lower part of body

Lower chamber or ventricle

FIGURE 10 — HEART CUT LENGTHWISE
THROUGH THE RIGHT SIDE

The left side of the heart pumps the blood all over the body, whence it returns to the heart again, but to the right side. The right side of the heart pumps the blood only into the lungs, whence it also returns to the heart, but to the left side.

Thus you see there is really a double circulation of the blood, and the heart is a double pump.

The pipes leading *from* the heart are called **arteries**. They are held wide open by muscles in their walls. They branch and branch, growing smaller and smaller as they

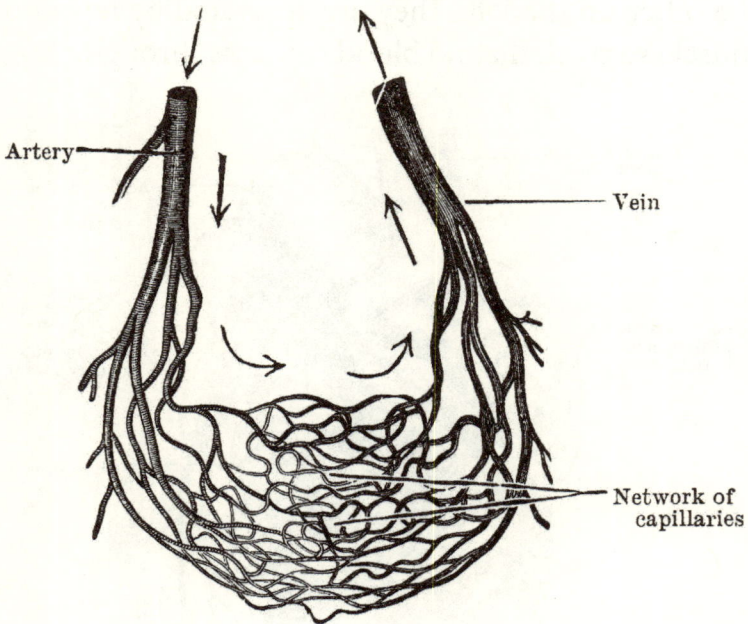

FIGURE 11 — DIAGRAM SHOWING HOW ARTERIES,
CAPILLARIES, AND VEINS ARE CONNECTED

do so. As they get smaller their walls get thinner, and at last we have pipes so minute that they cannot be seen by the naked eye. These, owing to their fineness, are called **capillaries**—from the Latin **capillus**, a hair (Figure 11). Their walls are so thin that gases and liquids can pass through them. We have already seen the capillaries at work, both in the food-pipe—absorbing the food as fast as it is dissolved, and in the lungs—taking in the fresh air and expelling the carbon dioxide.

The pipes leading *to* the heart are called **veins**. They are soft and fall together when empty. Starting from the capillaries, the veins, at first very small, are connected up into larger and larger tubes, until we have two great veins—one from the upper and one from the lower part of the body—which pour the blood into the heart.

Both sides of the heart are divided into an upper chamber, the **auricle**, and a lower chamber, the **ventricle** (Figure 10). On both sides the blood enters the auricle, while it is pumped onwards by the ventricle.

Between these two chambers is a floor of tough membrane so arranged as to form little trap-doors. These trap-doors open downwards very easily, and so let the blood pass from the auricle to the ventricle. As the ventricle fills, the trap-doors rise and close. They cannot be pushed upwards into the auricle by the pressure of the blood, for they are attached to the walls of the ventricle by very strong cords of membrane, which will only allow them to rise sufficiently high to make a level floor.

This prevents too great a rush of blood into the ventricle, and also prevents any possibility of the blood finding its way back into the auricle again. When the ventricle is full it contracts, and so pushes on the blood into the arteries.

Course of the Blood

In order to make the circulation quite clear to you, let us, in a short outline, follow the flow of the blood from the left ventricle round its double course and back again.

As it pours out of the left ventricle it is bright scarlet, for it is full of oxygen. It is driven by the pumping of the heart into a great artery, the **aorta**, which gives off branches to every part of the body. It speeds through the arteries easily, but when the capillaries are reached it moves slowly. Through the delicate walls of the capillaries the oxygen and the food pass out into the tissues, while the waste matters pass into the blood. Thus it is in the capillaries that the blood loses its scarlet colour and becomes purple.

Partly pushed onwards by the flow of more blood from the heart, and partly forced along by the movement of surrounding muscles, the blood now enters the veins and makes its way through them back to the heart again. Charged with waste matter, it enters the right side of the heart by the right auricle.

This is called the **general** circulation. Notice that here the arteries contain scarlet-red blood, full of oxygen, and the veins purple blood deprived of oxygen.

The blood now passes into the right ventricle, and is pumped into an artery which goes to the lungs. When it reaches the capillaries of the lungs, it gets rid of the carbon dioxide and some other waste matters, and takes in the oxygen of the air. Then it passes, scarlet-red once more, into a vein which pours it into the left side of the heart. This is called the **pulmonary** or lung circulation. Here the arteries contain the purple and the veins the scarlet blood.

This is the general scheme of the circulation, to which, however, you will find there are many details to be added if you ever go further into this subject.

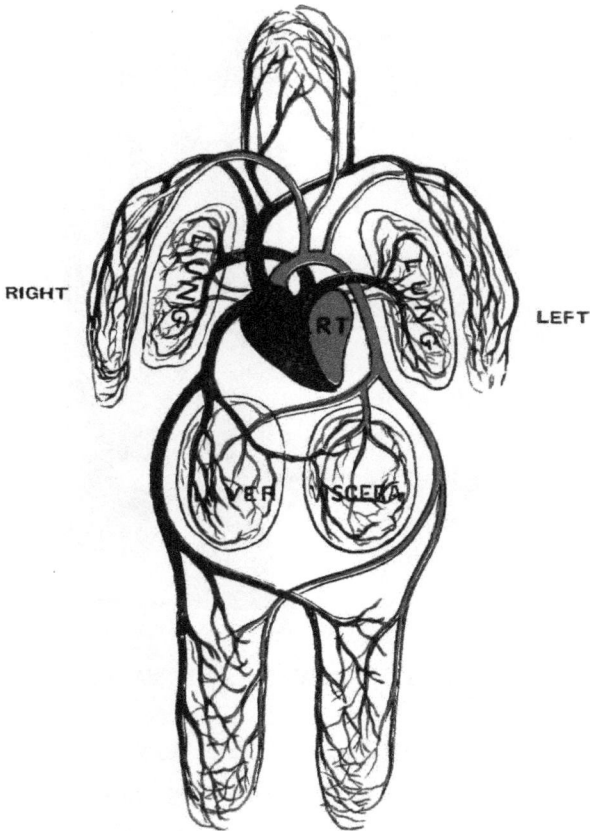

RIGHT   LEFT

PLATE II — DIAGRAM OF THE CIRCULATION

The purified blood (red) is seen in the left side of the heart, whence it is carried by the arteries upwards to both arms and both sides of the head and downwards to the liver and other internal organs (the viscera), and to the two legs. From the arteries it passes into the tiny blood-vessels called capillaries, and thence (now blue) into little veins, and so into larger veins upwards and downwards to the right side of the heart. It is then pumped into the lungs and returns to the left side of the heart to begin its course again.

Vein laid
open
Pockets or
valves

Direction
of flow.

Pockets or
valves

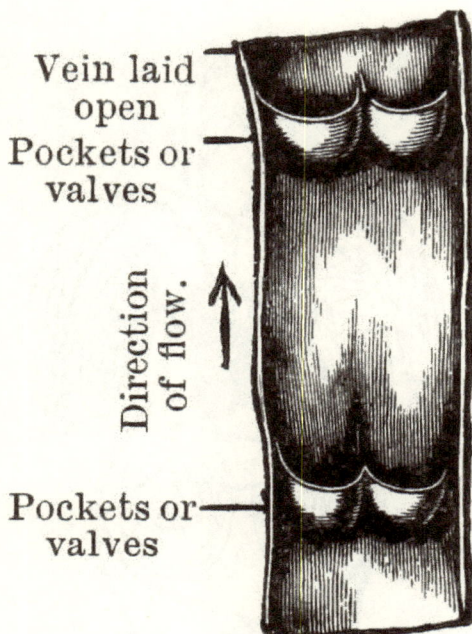

FIGURE 12 — A VEIN AND VALVES

In thinking of the blood and of its work in the body, you should not forget that the arteries and the veins are merely channels for the flow of the blood. It is only when in the capillaries that it can nourish the tissues and give them energy and heat. Hence practically every part of our bodies is crowded with capillaries.

If you could examine carefully the inner wall of a vein, you would see, at intervals, little valves or pockets, so placed that the opening is towards the heart (Figure 12). When the blood is coursing in the proper direction, it presses these tight against the wall of the vein, where they lie so close as to be no obstruction. The purpose of these valves is to prevent the blood in the

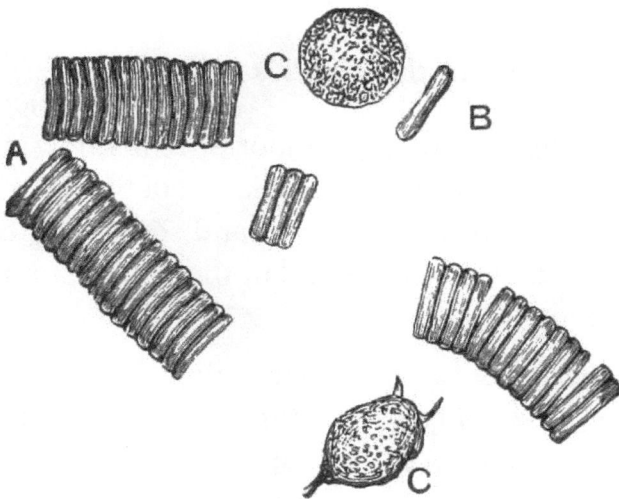

FIGURE 13 — BLOOD CORPUSCLES

A, rolls of red corpuscles;
B, isolated red corpuscle;
C, white corpuscles.

veins from flowing backward. If the current is stopped or forced back, the blood begins to find its way into the opening of the pockets, and by filling them forces them out further and further, till they form a barrier across the vein which the blood cannot pass. You can understand how a number of these valves closing the vein must prevent the blood from pressing back upon the capillaries. It is thus ensured that blood travelling towards the heart should not, through any accident, flow back let us say, into the feet.

I must tell you that similar pockets are placed in the great arteries near the heart to prevent any return of the blood to the ventricles.

What the Blood is Made Of

Although it is of great importance to know at least the general outline of the circulation of the blood, it is yet more important to understand something of the nature of the blood itself and of the service it renders to the body.

When looked at through the microscope, the blood is seen to be composed of three distinct substances: first, a clear colourless fluid called the **plasma** and then, floating in this, many millions of minute red bodies called the **red corpuscles**, and a somewhat smaller number of whitish bodies called the **white corpuscles** (Figure 13). The word corpuscle comes from the Latin **corpusculum**, a small body.

Of these three kinds of substance in the blood the plasma and the red corpuscles are the most important. It is the plasma which carries the food round the body, supplying nourishment to all the tissues, and taking from them all the matters they require to get rid of.

The work of the red corpuscles is of another kind. These have a regular form, that of round flat discs somewhat thickened at the edges; and, in shed blood, most of them are seen adhering together in groups looking like piles of tiny coins. These are the carriers of oxygen. As they pass through the lungs, the substance which gives them their red colour eagerly absorbs the oxygen in the air-sacs, and by the time they have passed out of the lungs the red corpuscles are saturated, that is, are filled as full as they can hold, with oxygen.

As you know, this oxygen, carried by them in the blood-stream through all the parts of the body, maintains that burning to which we owe heat and energy, and therefore life itself.

You will ask what work the white corpuscles perform. Under the microscope these appear as irregularly shaped particles of jelly-like matter. The purposes they serve are not yet fully known; but it seems that when anything injurious finds its way into the blood, it is the business of these corpuscles to attack and destroy it.

When any part of the body has been wounded or damaged, the white corpuscles flock to it in great numbers, and assist in keeping the tissues free from harmful foreign substances until they have been able to rebuild the parts that have suffered hurt.

The white corpuscles are in reality cells of living substance or protoplasm which have not formed tissue, but are free, and wander about in all parts of the body. There are numbers of them in the lungs and in the intestines, besides those in the stream of the blood.

Three Things Necessary for a Good Circulation

There is nothing more necessary for vigour and health than a good circulation. If our heart pumps steadily and strongly, and our blood courses swiftly through arteries, capillaries, and veins, then the oxygen we breathe in is carried rapidly to all the tissues and gives them energy, and the food we have eaten is quickly supplied to them, to repair waste and to help them to grow.

If the blood circulates too feebly we have a sense of weakness and fatigue due to the oxygen not being supplied freely enough and to the waste of the tissues not being soon enough repaired.

In order to keep the blood pure and to have it sent in a strong and rapid current through the body, three things are necessary.

First, we must eat good food and have enough of it—enough, but not too much; secondly, we must breathe fresh air, so that the blood which is being sent round the lungs may be thoroughly charged with oxygen; and thirdly, we must take sufficient exercise, for we must remember that the heart is a muscle, and as you may see in the chapter on bones and muscles, the great thing a muscle needs is exercise. When, by means of a little extra rapid movement, our whole body is thrown into greater activity, the heart shares in this general quickening up, and works more vigorously. Of course, it is important not to over-exercise, but in that respect exercise is only like everything else—we need good sense and judgment in our use of it.

Wounds

It may be useful just to mention what we ought to notice if ever we have to bind up a deep cut which has gone down below the capillaries next the skin and severed some larger blood-vessel.

If the blood flows in a trickle, and is dark red in colour, we may know that a vein has been cut. We should, of course, bind such a wound on the side **furthest** from the heart.

If the blood flows rapidly, is of a bright scarlet-red, we know that the cut has laid open an artery, and so, in order to stop the bleeding, the pressure of the bandage must be on the side **nearest** the heart. This latter is usually the more serious wound of the two.

CHAPTER V

THE EXCRETORY ORGANS

"East and West and North and South
Wash thy skin and close thy mouth."
— Rudyard Kipling

It is now time to tell you further how we get rid of the waste matter which is collected by the blood in its course through the body. This waste matter consists of gases, liquids, and solids. The principal gas, the carbon dioxide, goes out, as we saw, by the lungs. The liquid matter containing waste substances passes out by the lungs, the kidneys, and the outside and inside skin.

The Kidneys

We will take the kidneys first (Figure 14). These are two dark-coloured, bean-shaped bodies, which lie each on a cushion of fat. They are situated in the abdomen, behind the mass of the intestine, one on either side of the body in the region called the loins, above the hip-bones. From each of them passes a pipe leading to a bag or bladder, which communicates with the exterior by another pipe.

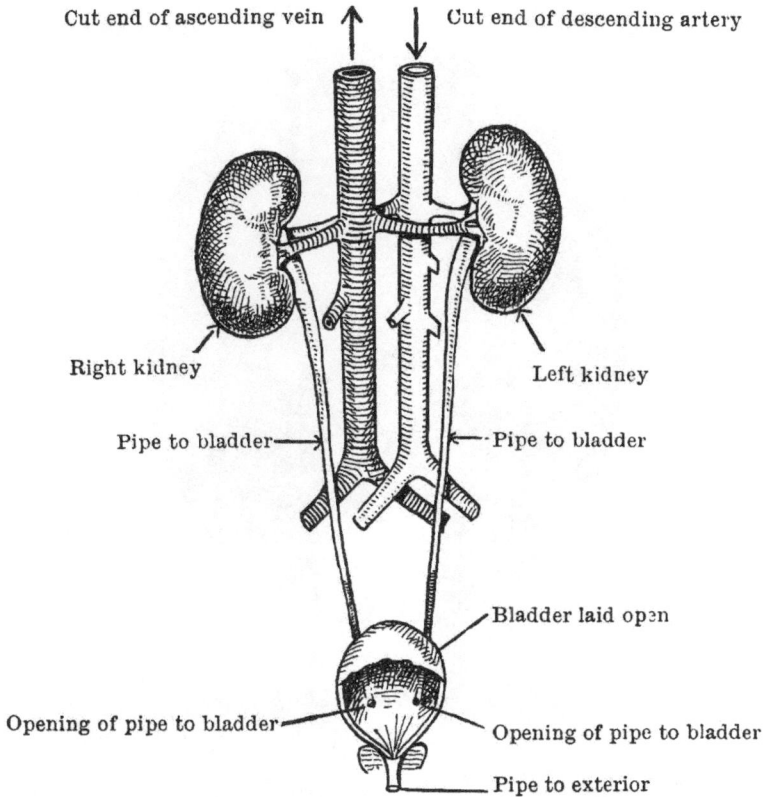

Cut end of ascending vein ↑ ↓ Cut end of descending artery

Right kidney

Left kidney

Pipe to bladder→ ←·Pipe to bladder

Bladder laid open

Opening of pipe to bladder

Opening of pipe to bladder

Pipe to exterior

FIGURE 14 — KIDNEYS AND BLADDER

I daresay you have seen the kidneys of sheep, which are often used as food. Next time you have the opportunity look at them carefully, and observe their shape, and also how exceedingly close is their texture. You would hardly believe that under the microscope the kidneys are seen to be composed of a number of extremely fine tubes.

This was first discovered by an Italian named Marcello Malpighi, who was the first man of science to

FIGURE 15 — MARCELLO MALPIGHI

study the parts of living things with the microscope. You can imagine what a number of wonderful discoveries he made. He lived in the seventeenth century, a time when all the learned men of Europe were growing very eager about science; but the curious thing is that the doctors of those days were not at all pleased with him, and said that it was a mistake to use the microscope for anything concerning the human body. However, by-and-by they found out their mistake, and now it is well known that no instrument ever invented has done even half as much as the microscope to enable men to understand their own bodies, and how to keep them in health.

Well, to go back to the kidney: I cannot attempt to describe to you what has here been discovered by the microscope, but you may remember that the fine tubes I mentioned just now secrete certain substances from the capillaries which run alongside them. This will at once tell you that the kidney is a kind of gland. It does not, however, secrete any substance which is to be of use; it secretes chiefly water, and what is called **urea**, which is waste matter containing useless nitrogen brought by the blood from all parts of the body. This watery substance, called **urine**, is sent down the pipe into the bladder; and from time to time, as the bladder becomes filled, its muscles contract and expel the urine.

The work that the kidneys perform is an exceedingly important one—in fact, if they are prevented from acting for any length of time death must result, for the waste matter which they collect and cast out will then choke and poison the body.

Hence we must be careful not to injure the kidneys; and there are three pieces of advice which I must give you concerning them: First, be cautious about exposure to cold and damp, and more especially after any violent exercise, or if you happen to be recovering from an illness. Secondly, do not wear tight clothes or tight belts, for being pressed or squeezed is very bad indeed for the kidneys. And thirdly, do not take alcohol, as you will see later on that this is apt to do them serious mischief. It is also as well to know that too much protein in our bodies means more waste nitrogen and harder work for the kidneys.

The Skin

But unceasingly as the lungs and the kidneys are working, and great as is the quantity of waste matter they cast out, they cannot by themselves get through all there is to be done. If they did not receive help they could not prevent our bodies from being choked and poisoned after all.

And so we come to the work of the skin.

The skin, as you know, is the covering which goes over the whole body. In an ordinary way it is the only part of a plant or an animal presented to the eye; and you will find it very amusing to count up all the different kinds of skins you have seen or heard of.

You remember that the whole body of an animal is nothing but cells of living substance or protoplasm, and that these cells grow into different shapes and alter their substance in various ways according to the work that they perform. All animals have not their bodies made in exactly the same way; but each has a body suitable for its own special needs.

Now, no part of an animal's body furnishes us with such marvellous instances of this as the skin. For from the cells of the skin are made the glittering scales of fish, the hard, rough scales of the crocodile or the lizard, the feathers of birds, some so soft and downy, others so long and firm, and the furry coats of quadrupeds. How different from one another in appearance are the wool of a sheep, the bristles of a hedgehog, and the short, smooth hair of a greyhound; yet these all are only parts of the skin. And we must not forget the beauty which adorns the skins of so many creatures. You will think of goldfish, of humming-birds and peacocks, of the tiger with his splendid stripes of tawny orange, and perhaps of the shining coat of a fine horse or the pretty brown fur of the squirrel. But the skin does more than afford an animal covering, protection, and warmth; it also gives it many of its weapons. Did you know that teeth and tusks and horns are not, for the most part, true bones, but are formed by the cells of the skin? Even such great weapons as the tusks of an elephant and the horns of a bull are made from the skin. Perhaps we may think that man is not so well provided as other animals are in this respect; still, his skin supplies him with teeth, with hair and with nails, as well as with a tough, waterproof, elastic covering for his whole body.

Can you tell me anything else there is in the skin? If you were to shut your eyes and I were then to take your hand, you would know it at once and how? You would **feel** it. The skin of your hand, in common with the skin of your whole body, is crowded with the ends of nerves, and you know that it is by means of our nerves and the messages they flash to the brain that we are enabled to see, hear, and feel. The skin, then, through the presence of these nerves, is the seat of the sense of touch.

Do these nerves go to every part of the body? You can tell me that by considering whether there is any part of the body which does not hurt us when cut. Oh, yes, you will instantly say, there are our hair and our nails. Quite right—into these our nerves do not go. Nor do they go in equal numbers to all parts of the skin. The skin of the back has the fewest nerves, the skin of the finger-tips the greatest number. And I think we may say that our wonderful finger-tips quite make up to us for not having in our skin such formidable weapons, or such brilliant colours, or such a cosy protection for our bodies as some animals have. And if you will stop for a minute or two, and think over what the finger-tips of man have accomplished, you will readily see what I mean.

The Skin of the Hand

Let us look for a moment at the skin of your hand. We will begin with the back of the hand. Passing your fingers over it, you may feel that the skin here is fairly smooth. If you hold it up to the light you may see that it has soft, downy little hairs scattered upon it, whilst if you look closely at the surface you will probably perceive a few small white flakes lying loose. You can pinch the skin up; this shows you that it is elastic.

What you see on the back of the hand is more or less what the skin is like over the whole of your body.

Now turn the hand over, and look at the palm and at the inner side of the fingers. You will notice first that the skin is somewhat smoother here than on the back of the hand and next that it has no hairs upon it. On looking closer you will see that the surface is all covered with very small ridges and furrows, which look like lines running across it. We shall find out in a moment how this appearance is caused. It is best marked on the finger-tips, and no two persons have these markings exactly alike. Rub the tip of your thumb in a little black lead from a pencil, or in a little soot, and then press it on white paper. There you will have your thumb-mark; no other thumb in the world can make one exactly like it. A man of science named Francis Galton was the first to study these finger-marks, and to discover that there are no two alike. Besides being very curious in itself, this discovery has been found useful as a means of identification, or of proving who a person is.

We cannot see much more than this with the naked eye, but if you will look at Figure 16 it will show you a section of the skin—that is to say, what you would see if you cut right down through it and then examined a very thin slice through a microscope.

You see at the top a number of rows or layers of cells, of which the very uppermost are flattened, the lower ones being more rounded. These layers form the **epidermis**, or overskin. They are quite white, and no blood-vessels run up into them. As fast as the inner cell-layers of the epidermis grow, they push against and flatten the outer layers, which die off and peel away in flakes. These are the loose flakes you saw on the back of your hand and in this manner the topmost layer of the epidermis is always coming away all over our bodies. Snakes cast their skins whole; but we, you see, are for ever casting ours in little bits.

Our epidermis is of very great service to us; it protects from injury the true skin underneath, and it

Opening of duct of sweat glands.

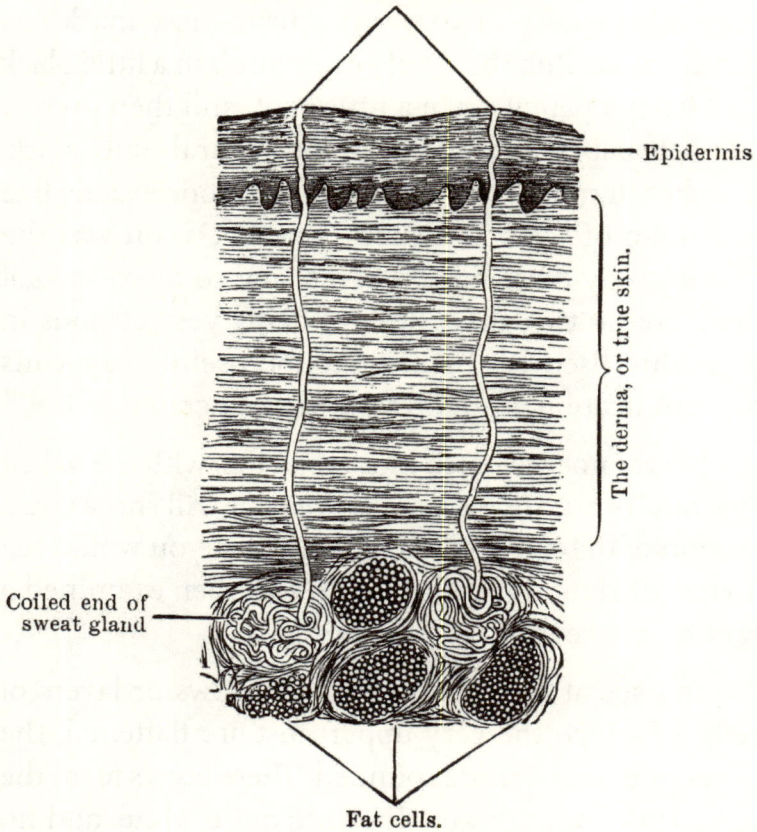

Epidermis

The derma, or true skin.

Coiled end of
sweat gland

Fat cells.

FIGURE 16 — A SECTION OF SKIN

helps to keep the temperature of our bodies even. It is
not of the same thickness everywhere, being thickest
at the heel. This thickness is caused by the constant
pressure and friction the heel has to endure; and in
the same way the epidermis of the palms of the hands
may grow thick, or as we say, horny, by doing a great
deal of hard or rough work. If we rub the epidermis too
much in any part which is not accustomed to friction,

a watery fluid gathers underneath it and forms a blister.

I must tell you that Malpighi discovered that the epidermis of the black man is of the same colour as a white man's—the darker hue of his skin being caused by a layer of colouring matter between the epidermis and the true skin.

The Inner Skin

If we tear off a piece of white skin from our hand, we lay bare a much softer pink skin beneath. This is the **derma** or true skin, and its pink colour is due to its being crowded with capillaries.

The first thing we notice in the true skin is that its upper surface is not one level, but is covered with little upstanding projections between which the epidermis comes down. The projections are called **papillæ**, and up into them run the capillaries, whilst some of them contain those nerve-endings which give us the sense of touch. These papillæ are most numerous in the palm of the hand and the finger-tips, and there they are arranged in rows. These rows make those tiny ridges and furrows, which you can print off as your thumb-mark or finger-marks.

Looking at the next diagram (Figure 17) you will have guessed that the long straight object which starts from a kind of pocket in the lowest part of the true skin is a hair. Notice the little bag-like projection at the side; this is an oil-gland which secretes a fatty substance, that is poured out through the opening made by the growth

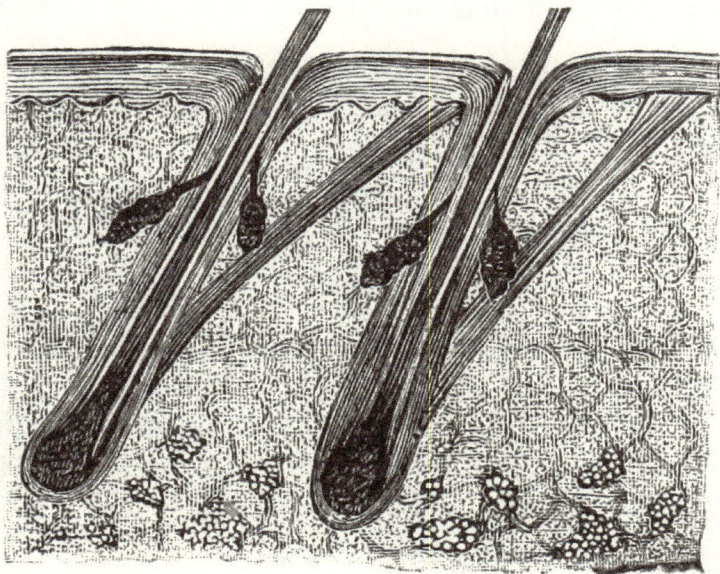

FIGURE 17 — A SECTION OF THE SKIN OF THE HEAD,
WITH HAIRS.

of the hair, and serves to keep the skin soft and supple. The feathers of birds and the fur of quadrupeds grow from the skin in the same way as our hairs do.

The Sweat-Glands

And how does the skin assist in getting rid of the waste matter of the body?

You may see in the epidermis a little opening, or pore, which goes by a spiral duct some way down into the true skin and there makes itself into a curious little coil. This is a **sweat-gland**. We have sweat-glands opening thus through our skin in nearly every part of our bodies.

In this diagram the sweat-gland is shown without the network of capillaries round it, for if this were put in, the coils of the gland would hardly be perceived. You have already been told how glands secrete, so that I need hardly say that through its thin wall, and through the thin wall of the capillaries close by it, the sweat-gland takes up into itself a watery substance from the blood, which is known as sweat or perspiration, and is really waste matter that the blood is eager to get rid of.

On a hot day, or when we have been taking violent exercise, we are aware of this perspiration; we may feel it trickling upon our foreheads, and making our hands wet. It is not then alone that we are perspiring; all day long and all night long the sweat-glands are drawing the watery fluid off from the blood and casting it out through the skin. They are somewhat less active in winter than in summer; still, the amount of sweat which is thus expelled from the body of a healthy man during an average twenty-four hours comes to about three pints. When the sweat-glands work more, the kidneys work rather less; and when the sweat-glands are comparatively inactive, the kidneys make up for it with increased activity.

If you consider that the lungs exhale watery vapour, that the urine is in great part water, and that the sweat is water also, you will begin to realize how much water we must take into our bodies. Indeed water forms a large proportion even of our solid food. It is good for us that it should be so; we need plenty of liquid substance within us to wash out and carry off impurities, and to keep our bodies supple.

Perspiration Poisonous

And now I am sure someone will ask, What becomes of all this perspiration? Yes, indeed, what becomes of it all?

Some of it is evaporated, that is to say, goes off as invisible steam into the air, through the holes of our clothing; some of it is caught by the clothing and stays upon it and some is left upon the skin.

Now, perspiration is poisonous; it is very harmful to let it collect upon our skin, or to wear clothes which are saturated with it. Moreover, the fat from the oil-glands is apt to mingle with the loose scales of the outermost layer of epidermis, and with these and any tiny bits of wool or cotton from our clothing, and with dirt from the atmosphere, it may form a thin crust over the skin. This is bad in two ways: first, because it stops up the openings or pores of the sweat-glands and prevents them from working freely; and secondly, because this coating of dirt is always ready to decompose or decay and then the decomposing matter gives off a most offensive smell.

Importance of Cleanliness

What is the remedy for this? The simple remedy is: keep your skin clean—wash. Once at least every day, every part of your skin should be well washed with soap and water, and rubbed down briskly with a roughish towel. The most comfortable way of doing this is to get into a bath—still, a basin of really hot water, with soap, a piece of flannel, and a towel, will do the necessary part of the business for us perfectly well, especially if we can contrive to have a good hot bath once a week. We must be particularly careful to wash thoroughly the armpits, all folded parts of the skin where dirt can easily collect, the parts surrounding the opening at the end of the food-pipe, and also the feet.

A wash all over every day freshens up the skin and keeps it healthy; it makes the blood circulate better, and the muscles stronger and it makes our minds brighter and more ready for good hard work and for vigorous play. You will find that all the men who are heroes in football or cricket or rowing know very well the value of a fresh, clean skin—know very well that if their bodies are clogged with waste matter that cannot get away, they must lose something of their strength and activity—and that may mean a beating.

After violent exercise especially, we should make a point of having a good rub down. The danger of catching cold after exercise comes from the fact that, when evaporation is taking place rapidly on the surface of any heated body, that body gets chilled very suddenly. So when we are very hot, and covered with perspiration, the perspiration, evaporating quickly, chills us: and the suddenness of the chill may do us serious injury. But if, before being chilled in this way, we rub ourselves clean and dry, we have removed the source of the danger.

But it is not enough to keep the skin itself clean; we

must take care that our clothes are clean also. Besides having them washed often enough, and changing them from time to time, it is a good thing to remember two little rules for every day. One is: Never, if you can help it, sleep at night in any garment you have worn during the day. And the other is: When you take off your clothes, shake them out well, and spread them, if possible, near an open window; the air playing upon them will then make them fresh and sweet again.

Effect of Foods upon the Skin

The kinds and amount of food we eat have an effect upon the skin. Too much meat is bad for it; so are pastries and rich cakes, and so is overdrawn tea. Worst of all is alcohol, which injures the nerves and the capillaries in the skin, and if persisted in makes the skin as a whole unhealthy.

The foods which act most favourably on the skin are fruit and fresh vegetables. Every girl and boy who reads this must have heard of the great Captain Cook and his voyages round the world. Besides being a man of great courage and ability, he was also exceedingly kind and tenderhearted, and he was very sorry for the seamen, who, in the long voyages of those days, before there were steamships, suffered dreadfully from a disease called scurvy, which begins in the skin. It is caused by the lack of fresh food, and it has cost many and many a seaman his life. It was Captain Cook who first found out how to prevent it, and this he did by bestowing immense care upon the feeding of his crews,

FIGURE 18 — CAPTAIN COOK

and by procuring quantities of fruit and vegetables for them at every place they touched. He also took pains to have every part of the ships kept perfectly clean. At the end of his second voyage, which lasted three years and eighteen days, he refers with a just pride to the "uncommon good state of health experienced by my people";—and if you have not yet read Captain Cook's journal of his voyages round the world, you should get the book out of a library and see his account of the measures he took. It is a splendid and exciting book in other ways besides, and I envy the boy or girl who sits down to read it for the first time.

If we take care of the skin, both by keeping it clean and by eating the right kind of food, we shall not only preserve it in good working order we shall also be warding off the attacks of innumerable enemies, invisible to our eyes, which are always floating about in the air around us, and like nothing so much as a good patch of dirt to settle in.

But of these I must tell you in another chapter.

CHAPTER VI

MUSCLES, BONES, AND JOINTS

"What a piece of work is a man . . . in form and moving how express and admirable!"

— SHAKESPEARE

Muscle

THE physical exercise which is necessary to make us strong and active is, in itself, exercise of the muscles and bones of the body, and in this chapter I must tell you something about these.

You may remember, in the account of the cells and their division of labour, that certain cells in the bodies of animals took upon themselves the work of contracting and expanding, and that these, being arranged in masses of tissue, by that contraction and expansion produced the movements of the body. Other cells, as we also saw, took upon themselves the making of a hard framework, which forms what we call the skeleton. In human beings, as in all the back-boned animals, this is found inside the softer tissues of the body, and consists of gristle or

cartilage, which, in the process of growth, is further strengthened by a chalky matter known as lime salts, and by degrees becomes **bone**.

No doubt you have often felt the biceps muscle swell up in your upper arm as you raised your hand towards your shoulder. On the inside of the elbow-joint you have also felt the hard cord which joins that muscle to the skin covering the bones of the lower arm, and pulls them up when the muscle contracts. Such a cord, as you have probably learnt, is called a **tendon**. It is the continuation of a fibrous sheath which wraps over the whole of the muscle.

You will now perhaps ask me what a muscle looks like. The lean of meat is muscle, and by examining it you may see that it consists of bundles of fibres or threads. These are themselves of no great length, but they are held together in what is often a considerable mass. On looking closer at the part of a muscle adjoining a bone, you may see the sheath which encloses it. This wraps every separate bundle of fibres as well as the whole muscle.

Muscles are of many different sizes and shapes, and you cannot form a good idea of them by thinking only of that muscular tissue which you may see exposed for sale as meat. This is all cut across and thus spoilt. A somewhat better notion may be gained by looking at the entire dead body of some small animal, such as a rabbit, after the skin has been removed. You can thus see the muscles left in place, each still covered by its sheath. But even so you will not be able to understand the beauty and flexibility of living muscle, which we can only guess at by observing its action, whether in human beings or in animals. You have no doubt often watched kittens at play, or the flight of swallows, or fish swimming in a pool; you have seen a strong horse pulling a waggon uphill, and noticed the play of the great muscles of the haunches; and I daresay many of you who read this have practised your own muscles in various ways—perhaps you can turn catherine-wheels, vault a five-barred gate, and swarm up a rope. When you are trying to form some idea of a muscle it is better to think chiefly of instances of muscular activity, such as these, rather than to keep in mind the muscle which you see as the lean of meat.

Voluntary and Involuntary Muscles

The muscles of which we have spoken hitherto are governed by our will, that is our brain. The nerve-endings in their fibres are connected by strands of nerve-tissue with that part of the brain which controls the movements and actions we are ourselves aware of. Hence these are called **voluntary** muscles. Besides these, we have a great number of muscles whose action we are not aware of, and cannot control, which are called **involuntary**. These are not quite the same in their structure and action as the voluntary muscles. They form the walls of the food-pipe, the walls of the arteries, and several other parts of the body.

The muscle which forms the heart is of a structure somewhat different from any other.

You have, of course, noticed that the lean of meat is red, and I think you must have guessed that this redness is caused by the blood in the capillaries. The capillaries pass into the muscles in great numbers, supplying them both with oxygen and with food to repair the waste of muscular tissue which exercise causes. No part of the body uses up energy and food so much as the muscles, hence you see the importance of good food and of fresh air if we wish our muscles to be strong. Do you know why a person gets out of breath with violent exercise? When the muscles are made to do hard work, they quickly use up the oxygen in the blood, depriving the brain of the oxygen it needs in order to control them. If the breathing is not deep and rapid enough to supply the brain with more, the person feels what we call "out of breath," and has to stop the exercise in order to draw in a sufficient supply of air. The deeper you breathe the better the play of your muscles will necessarily be.

The Diaphragm

But muscles themselves have a great deal to do with breathing; and so I must tell you a little about the chief ones concerned in it.

The most important of these are the muscles which unite to form the **diaphragm**. The word "diaphragm" means a partition, and our diaphragm is a partition dividing the chest—which contains the heart and the lungs—from the abdomen, which contains the stomach, intestines, and other organs. The diaphragm is, in fact, the muscular floor of the chest.

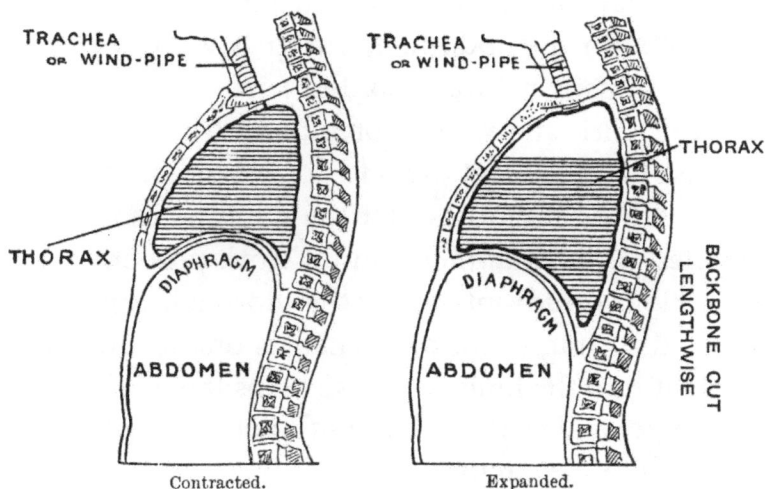

FIGURE 19 — THE CHEST CONTRACTED IN EXPIRATION
AND EXPANDED IN INSPIRATION

When the diaphragm expands, it sinks downwards, pressing upon the abdomen, and enlarging the space within the chest. At the same time, the muscles at the side of the chest expand, so that there is plenty of room for the lungs to be distended with air. Then the diaphragm contracts, as do also the muscles at the sides of the chest, and the air is forced out of the lungs again (Figure 19).

Now, deep breathing means exercising the diaphragm, expanding and contracting it well. If you observe what happens when you breathe as deeply as you can you will find that the muscles of the abdomen move quite as much as those of the chest; in fact, anyone who has been careful to practice abdominal, or deep, breathing will draw great breaths without any raising of the shoulders.

You may sometimes see it stated that boys and men breathe with the abdomen, but girls with the chest, and that this is naturally so. But such statements are not true. Girls and women breathe with the chest, not because nature meant them to do so, but because they wear such tight clothes that the diaphragm and the muscles of the abdomen cannot work properly. This is a serious disadvantage, for the thorough expansion of the diaphragm not only enables one to draw the air right into the lungs, but also helps the work of the food-pipe, makes the beating of the heart easier, and is helpful to the circulation.

So I advise my girl readers not to pinch themselves into tight stays and bodices, but to wear loose clothes which will leave the diaphragm room for proper activity.

You must know that the diaphragm is one of nature's latest improvements: a frog has none; birds have no more than the beginnings of one. It is only when we come to the mammals (that is, animals that suckle their young) that we find it fully formed; and those who do not take the trouble to exercise it properly are giving up the use of what has been a great help in the advance of the mammals. Do any of us wish to go back to the reptiles?

Bones

The backbone or spine itself, with the skull attached to the upper end of it, is the only part of the skeleton which we find in every backboned animal. All the rest is different in different creatures.

In examining a backbone, as you may easily do in any museum, you should notice the shape of the vertebræ, or small bones of which it is composed. You will observe that each consists of a thickish disc of bone, upon which is set a little arch. From the arch spring processes, mostly three in number, and somewhat different in shape in different animals, as well as in different vertebrae of the same backbone. The midmost of these is called the spine-like projection or **spinous process**; and if you run your hand down your own backbone, or that of any vertebrate animal, you will plainly feel the row of these spinous processes under the skin.

When the discs of the vertebræ are fitted in order, one upon the other, the holes beneath the arches also correspond exactly with one another, and so make a channel. Along this channel passes the **spinal cord**, protected by the backbone from chances of injury. You will learn in another chapter how important the spinal cord is.

The number of vertebræ is not the same in all vertebrate animals—but the principle of the backbone is always the same. In the living body the vertebræ are connected by means of ligaments, or bands of tissue, and between each of them is flexible cartilage, which enables the backbone to move, and acts like the buffers of a train in preventing shock.

Our own backbone has 33 vertebræ. Near the lower end five of them are welded together and form what is now practically one bone (Figure 20). Below this,

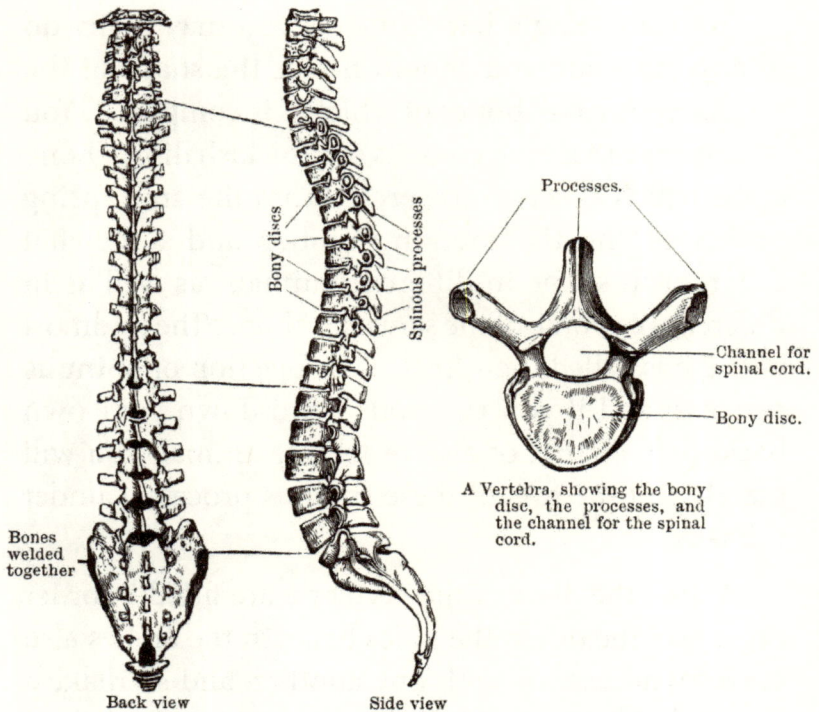

FIGURE 20 — THE SPINE

again, the four lowest vertebræ are joined together in a similar way, and form a much smaller mass which is the termination of the spine.

We find many animals having bones which branch out on either side of the spine, and serve to protect the internal organs from injury. These **ribs**, as we call them, may be seen in fish, and still better in snakes, which have them all down the backbone, from head to tail. On the other hand, we have animals in which the ribs have almost disappeared—such, for instance, as the frog.

In mammals the tendency is for the ribs to grow fewer. We ourselves have twelve ribs on each side;

of these the ten upper ones are joined in front by means of the gristly breastbone and thus make the chest, in which the heart and lungs are situated; the two last are smaller and their ends are not joined to the others nor to the breastbone.

Then, again, among the backboned animals we have some possessed of limbs and some without any. Those which have limbs must have them attached in some way to the backbone, and we find in some animals two bony girdles, one in front near the head, the other near the hinder end of the spine. On these are suspended the fore and hind legs respectively. Animals who use their fore-limbs for other purposes than walking may have **collar-bones** or **clavicles**, which keep the fore-limbs apart and enable them to move freely. Such, among others, are most birds and monkeys; and such are we ourselves.

The hinder girdle is small in many four-footed animals, but in monkeys we find it well developed, for when an animal holds itself erect as these can, the bones of this girdle have to support the abdomen. In ourselves it is still stronger in proportion.

You will find it most interesting to inquire how the bones of our legs and feet, and arms and hands, correspond with those of the limbs of four-footed animals. Where do you suppose are the joints in a horse which correspond to our wrist and knee?

Gristle

Now, it is most important to remember that in childhood and youth many parts of the skeleton are not yet true bone, but are soft gristle or cartilage. This bends easily; and if it is bent, the bone, as it slowly forms, will take the same shape and so be bent too. Hence we must be careful while we are young not to stoop and slouch; we must hold ourselves well so that the bones may grow straight and strong. And, more than this, we must be very careful of babies and small children whenever we have anything to do with them; for many people have suffered all their lives because those who had charge of them when they were very young forgot, or perhaps did not know, how delicate the framework of a baby's little body is. Little children often have bow-legs from being allowed to walk too soon—before their bones can support them. On the other hand, many children are wheeled about in perambulators when they should be exercising their legs.

Arches in the Human Body

Any girl or boy who knows a little about building has heard that an arch is one of the most useful of all forms employed in that work. Now Nature has provided us with an arch, which, like those used in building, is intended to support the mass above it. And our arch is the more remarkable because no other animal has one like it. Do you know where this arch is? It is the arch of the **instep** (Figure 25). When you stand firm upon the ground, you stand on the ball of the foot and toes, and on the heel; but the middle part of the sole of your foot does not touch the ground except along the outer side. It is this arch which gives spring to the walk and firmness when standing still, and it has always been reckoned the chief beauty of the human foot. So my advice to you is, do not spoil the arch of your instep. You will do so if you persist in wearing high heels and tight shoes.

Another arch we have is of a different kind. I mean the arch of the skull which encloses and protects the brain. This arch is exceedingly strong when fully developed, and in many countries heavy loads are carried upon it. In Germany and Switzerland you may often see countrywomen carrying on their heads enormous loads of hay or grass, or great baskets full of things by no means light of weight. This does not injure the skull, and it has the advantage of leaving the hands free, and of giving those who practise this method of carrying a very erect and graceful walk.

At the same time I must remind you that the skull is made up of several bones, some of which do not even meet until a child is about four years old. Moreover, all the parts of the skull are not equally thick. You may do a person very serious injury by a blow on the head and it is especially important to guard the heads of your little playfellows from being knocked in any way.

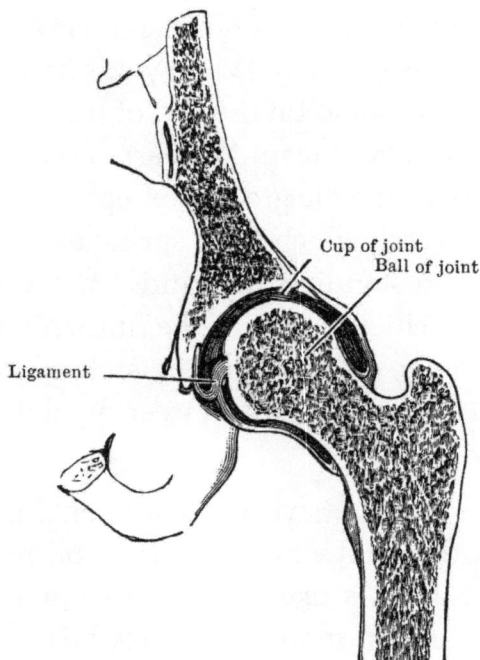

FIGURE 21 — CUP-AND-BALL JOINT
CUT THROUGH LENGTHWISE

Joints

I need not tell you that our bones are jointed one upon the other and thus enabled to perform a great number of movements.

In principle most of these joints are either cup-and-ball joints—such as those of the shoulder and hip, where the bones of the upper arm and upper leg are rounded into a knob, and play freely in a socket (Figures 21 and 22); or they are hinge-joints—as those of the elbow, the knee, and the fingers, where a projection of the one bone fits into a groove in the other (Figures 23 and 24).

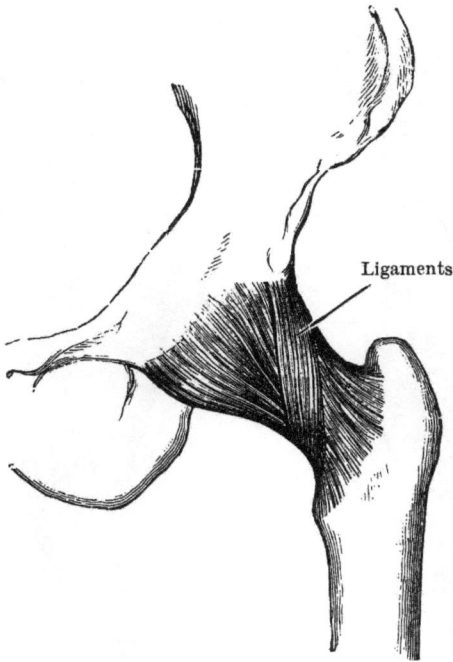

FIGURE 22 — EXTERNAL VIEW OF CUP-AND-BALL JOINT

You will ask how these joints are kept in place, They are held together by means of bands called **ligaments**, composed of a fibrous tissue, which we find in many parts of the body, serving to bind different organs or portions of an organ together, and hence called **connective tissue.**

No doubt it has already struck you as a wonderful thing that our joints should move over one another as silently as they do. This is made possible by the ends of the bones being covered with gristle, or cartilage, which in a living body is full of moisture, and most marvelously smooth. Besides this, a fluid substance

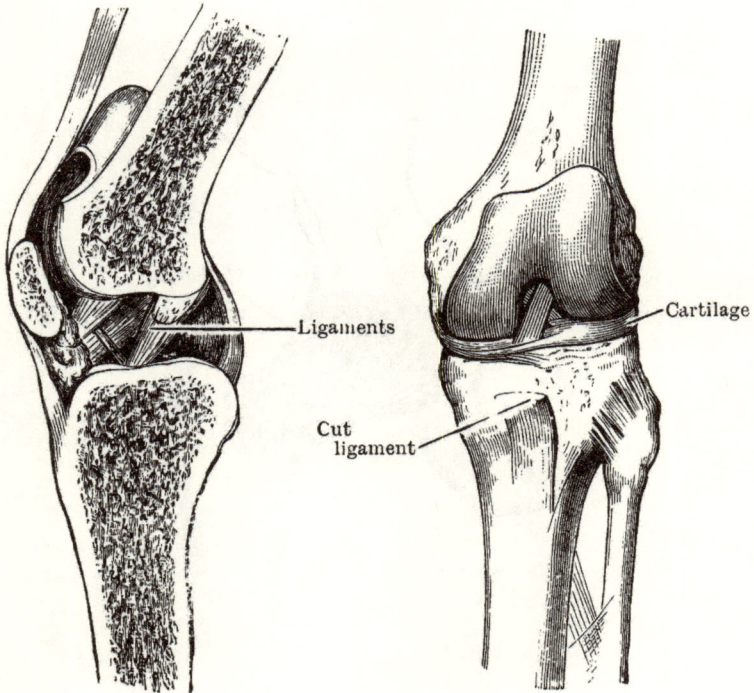

FIGURE 23 — HINGE
JOINT CUT THROUGH
LENGTHWISE

FIGURE 24 — EXTERNAL
VIEW OF HINGE JOINT

is being continually poured out over the ends of the
bones from underneath the ligaments which hold them
together. Hence, being both very moist and beautifully
smooth, the joint moves with the greatest ease and
without a sound.

There is one joint which I must tell you about
particularly: that by which the skull moves on the top
of the backbone. At the base of the skull is a hollow
ring of bone, which is really the first vertebra; this rests
round a bony peg rising from the second vertebra. The
ring rotates upon the peg, as on a pivot, when the head

is turned from side to side. You can try for yourself how far the head will go round. If this ring is moved off the peg the result is death; hence a child should never be lifted by the head, for the young bones and ligaments are still weak, and might thus be fatally displaced. It is also dangerous to swing children by the arms, lest the cup-and-ball joint be dislocated.

How Muscles and Bones Work Together

There is no single movement of the body, or of any part of it, which is performed by one muscle alone. We find this out when any muscle is hurt. For instance when one has a stiff neck, nearly every movement of the body is awkward and more or less painful, because so few movements of the body can be made without affecting the muscles of the neck.

Again, in order that one set of muscles may be active, some other set must remain inactive. Thus if your biceps muscle is active pulling up your forearm, it is partly owing to the fact that the muscle at the back of the upper arm is inactive.

This **co-ordination**, or harmonious working together of many bones and muscles, is one of the most wonderful facts of bodily life. When it is perfect we get ease, skill, and grace; when it is imperfect we are awkward and work with difficulty. There is nothing of greater advantage than to have one's muscles act in proper co-ordination, and you should remember two points about this.

LOWER END
THIGH BONE

TENDON

KNEE CAP

MUSCLE OF
LOWER LEG

BONES OF
LOWER LEG

TENDON

ANKLE BONE

TOE BONES

HEEL BONE

ARCH OF
INSTEP

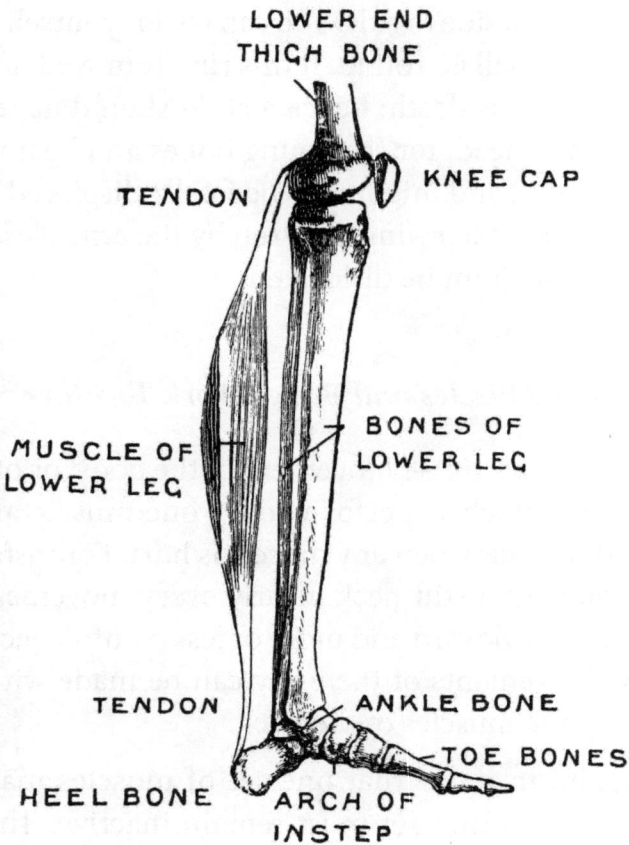

FIGURE 25 — BONES, MUSCLES, AND
TENDONS OF LOWER LEG AND FOOT

First, co-ordination is very much a matter of training and habit: hence we see little children, who to begin with are helpless in their hands and limbs, gradually acquire the use of them by exercise.

In the second place, the co-ordination of the muscles, and especially of the finer ones, is easily spoilt by laziness and intemperance. Hence a workman who drinks and a workman who habitually does work without care both lose their skill. Skill once lost is regained with great difficulty.

All our lives long we require exercise to keep this coordination at its best and among the many forms of exercise there is one which is of special advantage—1 mean, swimming. A moment's recollection of the movements required for swimming will make you realize what a number of muscles it calls into play; while besides increasing our muscular activity it is a great help towards cleanliness, and good for the lungs and the circulation. I need hardly say anything about its possible use in preserving one's own life, or enabling one to save another's—that must occur to everyone. I would urge every boy and girl who has not yet learnt to swim to set about it as soon as possible.

We should remember that it is not unusual violent exertion now and then which will develop the body well; it is the steady practice of good physical exercise for a short time every day; it is care to breathe deep and to get all the fresh air we can every day, and every day to choose plain and nourishing food rather than food which may tempt us more, but will not build up the body properly. These are the things which will make us grow up into strong men and women, with good straight bones, powerful muscles, and bodies capable of quick movement, grace, and skill.

CHAPTER VII

THE SENSE ORGANS

*"Health is not only to be well, but to be able to use well
every power we have."*

— Florence Nightingale

Unless we set ourselves deliberately to think about
it, we hardly realize how entirely we depend upon our
senses for what we are able to know and to do. They
have been called the "gateways of knowledge," since they
lead from the outer world to that inner world which
each one of us feels within himself. Without them we
can gain no information about the things around us,
nor can we direct our actions and it is through their use
that the brain has been gradually developed from the
first little cluster of nerve-cells, formed in very lowly
animals, upwards to the brain of man with its millions
of cells and fibres.

Senses of Lower Animals

As you will learn more fully in the next chapter,
there are no animals whose brain can be compared
with that of man; but there are many animals whose

108

senses are sharper and better than ours. You and I can neither see as well as a hawk or an eagle, nor smell as keenly as a dog. There are sounds in nature too high and too low for our ears to catch, which can be heard by our brother animals. For instance, the cat can hear the high, shrill notes of mice, which are inaudible to her mistress. As for the mice, they know when a cat is in the house by their sense of smell.

It would seem, moreover, as if the senses of civilised men were not on the whole so acute as those of uncivilized races, as you may find out for yourselves by reading accounts of peoples like the Native Americans of North America, or the blacks of Africa.

Origin of the Senses: Sight

We shall best understand the senses by considering one instance of how they first arose. I told you very briefly in another chapter how the first of them is the sense of touch, seated in the cells of the skin, and how the others were derived from it by means of division of labour among those cells.

Now, the first many-celled animals lived in the ocean. They were sensitive all over. They could feel whether anything they came in contact with was hard or soft, rough or smooth, good to eat or better avoided. They could also tell when anything came between them and the sun, for they felt the difference in the degree of heat; and they were aware of vibrations or movements in the water. But these sensations of theirs were indistinct, and they themselves were very defenceless.

After a time, certain of the touch-cells became sensitive to light only. These were clustered together; and the living substance within them made a pigment or colouring-matter, which absorbed instead of reflecting the rays of light. Nerve-threads connected the cluster with the chief nerve-cells of the body.

By degrees, as, through their work, they became more and more sensitive, these cells drew a little inwards from the surface of the body, and were arranged at the bottom of a sort of cup, lined with pigment. In front of them certain cells of the skin became transparent and formed a little lens. This collected the rays of light directing them straight upon the sensitive cells, which by this means had printed upon them an image—doubtless at first a blurred and faint one—of the world around.

This was the beginning of the eye, as we now find it in such animals as jelly-fish, starfish, wandering water-worms, and snails.

If you were to compare such lowly eyes as these part by part, with the human eye, you would find a great difference between them, for the human eye is not only much more complicated than this, but the cells which form it have a different history. Nevertheless, the principle of the eye is always the same. It is a little camera, in which certain cells collect the light, and by this means form a picture upon a sensitive surface behind them, kept in darkness—just as may be done with a photographic camera. And this camera communicates by nerves with the chief nerve-centre of the body.

The first eyes, as I have told you, were placed on or near the surface of the animal; but by-and-by they were sunk further within the body and protected in different ways. The form of protection we know best is that of a bony chamber or socket and eyelids, such as we have ourselves.

Hearing, Taste, and Smell

The development of the senses of hearing, taste and smell begins in the same way as does that of sight, viz., by certain touch-cells becoming sensitive to one kind of influence from the world around, and to no other, and gradually reaching a great perfection in their work, because they attend to it alone.

The nerve-endings which form the organ of the sense of **hearing** are sensitive only to movements in the atmosphere. These movements may be started by wind or water, by the fall of rocks and stones, by objects striking against one another or passing over the ground, and by the voices of animals and men. As the quiverings or **vibrations** in the air strike against the nerve-endings, these pass messages concerning them to the brain, where they are perceived as sounds, and distinguished one from another as being high or low, harsh or musical, and as coming from this or that direction.

The endings of the nerve-cells which are the organ

of the sense of **smell** can detect in the air the most minute particles derived from animals, plants, or any other object, and send reports of them to the brain, where they are recognized by those different effects which we call scents.

The nerve-endings which form the organ of the sense of **taste** act in a precisely similar manner, except that it is their business to send a report, not of minute particles floating in the air, but of substances dissolved in liquid which are brought into contact with them.

The Human Eye

We must now turn to our own sense-organs and see how they have improved upon the humble beginnings we have just been considering.

In the chapter on the skin you will find as much as is necessary for you to know at present about the sense of touch, so we will go on at once to the eye.

By far the best way of learning about it is to procure one or two ox eyes, and examine them for yourselves. This must be done with great care, for the structure of an eye is most wonderful and delicate. If you cannot do this at the moment you may understand something of the structure of the eye by looking at the plate facing page 114.

You will remember that there are three different parts in a complete organ of sight. There is the part which collects the rays of light and leads them to a definite spot or focus; there is the part which receives the image or picture made by these rays and a third, which communicates the sensation made by the image of the thing seen to the chief nerve-centre—in the higher animals and ourselves, to the brain. If any one of these three be missing, or greatly injured, there is no sight; but we should never forget that that which **sees** is not the eye itself, but that part of the brain which finally receives the message.

Let us first consider how the light is collected. Looking at the plate you will see that the eye bulges out somewhat in front. This part is covered by a membrane, horny and rather thick but perfectly transparent, known as the **cornea**, behind which lies a watery substance, called the **aqueous humour**. Passing through these the light falls upon that part which strikes us most when we look at an eye, the coloured ring, or **iris**, and the black hole, or **pupil**, at its centre. The iris acts as a circular curtain which can be opened wide or drawn together, so as to admit more light, or shut out an excess of it. This is done by marvellously fine involuntary muscle fibres. Immediately behind it is a most beautiful little object which, if you are examining a bullock's eye, you may detach from the delicate membrane in which it is slung, and hold separately in your hand. This is the **lens**, colourless, and as clear as the very clearest glass, somewhat rounded in front and behind. Save that it is moist, and not very hard, you might think you were holding a jewel. This is the instrument by which the light is collected, in exactly the same manner as by the lens of a photographic camera. This lens is made up of cells arranged in a very marvellous manner; in fact, you should never forget, in considering an eye, that the whole of it is composed of cells, altered in different ways to suit the different parts they have to perform. The lens can be adjusted to the needs of sight, so as to collect and focus the rays coming from objects near at hand as well as those coming from a distance.

Behind the lens lies what forms the mass of the eyeball—the **vitreous**, or **glassy humour**, a substance like a delicate jelly, which, being also transparent, allows the rays of light to pass through it unhindered.

These five, the cornea, the aqueous humour, the iris, the lens, and the vitreous humour, together form that part of the eye which collects, focusses, and gives a passage to the light rays.

Where Images are Formed

We have now to consider where the image is formed. You must not suppose that the little picture you may see by looking at the eye of a person is the image of what the person sees; that is merely the reflection from the surface of the cornea. We must look behind the vitreous humour to find the image.

The eyeball, as a whole, is covered with a tough, thick membrane of an opaque whitish colour, called the **sclerotic** (or hard) coat. We see some of it on either side of the iris, and call it the white of the eye. The cornea is really a continuation of it, made transparent over the region of vision. Now if we turn back the sclerotic coat we shall see that between it and the vitreous humour

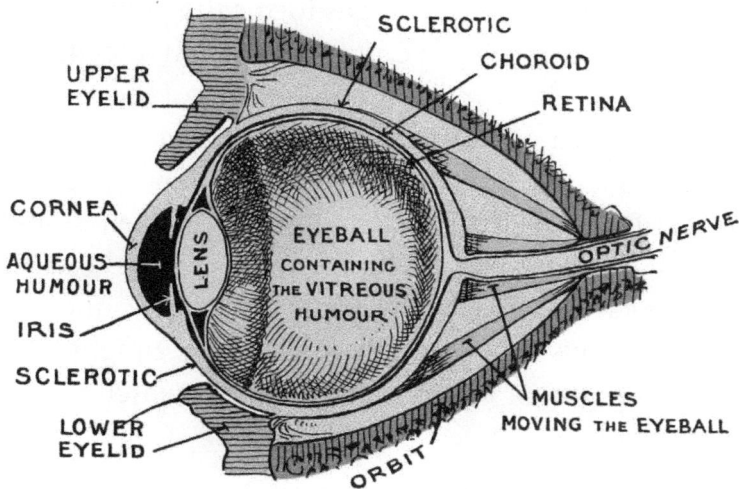

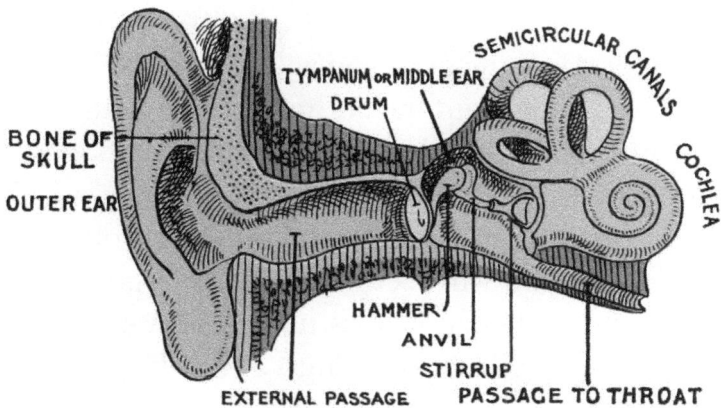

PLATE III — THE HUMAN EYE AND EAR

there is a layer of membrane, purplish black in colour, supplied with many capillaries on the inner surface. This, within the sclerotic, encloses almost the whole eyeball, except so much of it as forms the pupil within the iris; the iris itself is a continuation of it attached to a ring of very delicate muscles lying round the capsule, or little sheath of most delicate membrane, in which the lens is slung. This layer of purplish black is called the **choroid coat** (from the Greek **chorion**, membrane). You will guess that this dark pigment serves the same purpose as the darkness of the photographic camera in which the rays sent through the lens are caught. It is this dark pigment at the back of the eye which makes the pupil black.

But a lens and a dark chamber will not give us a picture—we must have besides something which corresponds to the sensitive plate of photography.

If you look at the plate you will see something like a stalk projecting from the outline of the eyeball. This is the **optic nerve**, which goes to the brain: in the plate for convenience, it is shown as cut through at a little distance from the eyeball. Now follow this through the sclerotic, and you will see that it does not go further than the choroid coat; it does not penetrate into the vitreous humour. It expands into a film-like layer of nerve-tissue of a very marvellous construction, which spreads itself over the inner surface of the choroid coat, and receives the image brought by the rays of light passing through the lens. This film-like layer is called the **retina** (a net). Whatever we see is in reality the picture thrown upon the retina and reported by the optic nerve to the centre of seeing in the brain.

Images Upside Down

Take a water-bottle of plain glass well rounded near the bottom, and fill it with water. Then place a sheet of white cardboard on one side of it and a lighted candle on the other, and you will see an image of the candle cast on the cardboard. The image will be clearer if you take a second piece of cardboard, make a hole in it, and place it between the burning candle and the bottle.

This will form a very good representation of what takes place in the eye; the water-bottle filled with water, serving as cornea, aqueous humour, lens, and vitreous humour all in one, and the cardboard with the hole in it taking the place of the iris. As for the cardboard on the other side of the bottle, that is doing duty as the retina. And what do you observe about the image on this pretended retina? It is upside down!

This is due to the path of the rays through the water; they are bent and cross one another, so that what was above is below and what was below is above. Is this the same with our eyes? Exactly the same. The image on the retina, the image conveyed to the centre of sight in the brain, is an inverted, or upside down, image; but the cells in the brain which receive it learn to turn it back again, so that we actually see things the right way up.

Is not all this very wonderful? You will understand that I have shown you only the merest outline of the eye; there are many more marvels for you to discover,

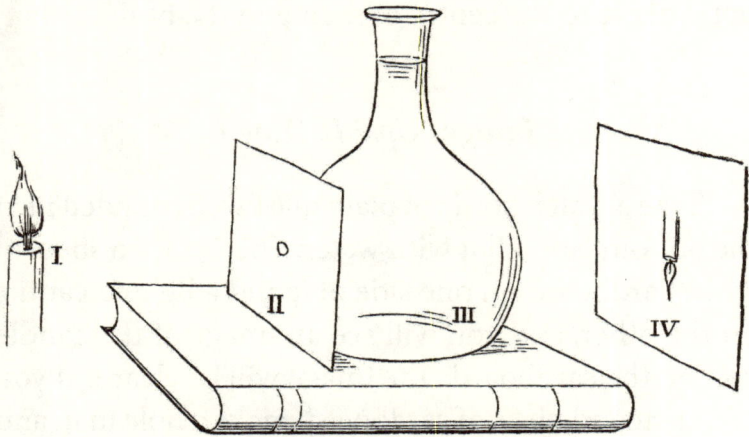

FIGURE 26 — EXPERIMENT TO SHOW HOW AN IMAGE
IS FORMED ON THE RETINA

  I. *the object looked at;*
 II. *cardboard with hole in it, representing the iris;*
 III. *water-bottle, representing the cornea, aqueous*
   humour, lens, and vitreous humour;
 IV. *cardboard representing the retina, with the*
   image upside down.

especially, perhaps, concerning the retina. I hope that some of you will not remain satisfied with what you have learnt here, but by-and-by, when you have thoroughly mastered this much, will go on and find out more.

How the Eye is Protected

Meanwhile, I must tell you a little about the manner in which this delicate organ is protected. You can pass your hand outwards along your brow and follow the edge of the bone down the side of the eye, and round underneath it till you get to your nose. This bony circle is the edge of the **orbit** in which the eye is placed, and which serves as its first protection. Close to the eyeball we have the eyelids, which are opaque, and which we can shut or wink in too strong a light and at their edges we have the eyelashes which are meant to keep out dust.

Within the eyelids are the four groups of muscles which move the eyeball: a group on each side, one above and one below. These muscles, like all others, are much improved by exercise. Those which lift the upper eyelid are often neglected.

On the outer side of the eyes, furthest from the nose, are the tear-glands, which secrete that salt, watery fluid we know so well. It was not originally meant for weeping, but for moistening the eye, so that it might be free from dirt, and that the cornea might be kept transparent. These tears are always flowing a very little, though we do not know it. On the inner side of each eyelid is a little canal leading to a duct or passage which passes into the nose, so that the tears do not fall over the lower eyelid unless one is weeping. They are poured forth plentifully from the gland, as you know, whenever anything gets into the eye, in order to wash it away. Now, since the duct is by the side of the nose, remember, if ever you get a fly or a bit of sand in your eye, to lift the upper lid and move it over the eyeball **towards** the nose, not away from it. Blowing the nose vigorously is also a help.

How to Take Care of Our Eyes

But though Nature has thus done a good deal to protect our eyes for us, there are several points that we ourselves must attend to if we wish to keep our sight good.

In the first place, you should remember that the eye till it is full-grown finds it a somewhat difficult matter to adjust the lens so as to make a clear picture on the retina. This difficulty is more particularly felt with objects close to the eye; and the younger the child, the more severe is the strain. Therefore do not let any little child you may have to take care of do fine needlework, or look at small letters in a book.

Generally speaking, books and work should be held about 10 to 12 inches from the eye. If at that distance they cannot be seen clearly, then the letters or stitches are too small for even a grown-up person's ordinary employment, and are exceedingly bad for children.

Overstrain of the eyes causes headache, squinting, nervous irritability, great fatigue, and a sort of stupidity due to not seeing properly. If the overstrain is prolonged, the sight may be injured for life.

If you have any difficulty about your sight, go and see an **oculist**—that is, a doctor who has made a special study of the eye. He will give you, if necessary, a prescription for glasses, which will not only make it possible for you to see better, but will also tend to correct, or at any rate will not increase, whatever defect he may find in your eyes. Never go to an **optician**, that is, to a spectacle-maker, **for advice**; for though he can test your sight he cannot tell what is actually wrong in the eye itself; and though the glasses he gives you may make you see better for a time, in the long run they may make your sight worse than ever. The proper business of the optician is to make the glasses ordered by the oculist.

The position of the light by which one is working or reading makes an immense difference to the eyes. You should never read with your face to the light. The best way is to sit with your back to it, arranging yourself in such a manner that it falls full upon the page, without the shadow of your head interfering. When writing or working, the light should be on the left, in order that the eyes may not be harassed by the moving shadow of the right hand.

These details, which at first sight may seem small, are in reality a most important part of the care of the eye. The principle is: Get full, steady light on whatever you are doing, but keep the eye itself in shadow. At the same time we should avoid looking long at surfaces which are glaring, such as a page in bright sunlight, as this fatigues the retina, and may injure the eye and nervous system.

As you know, people differ much in their sight. We cannot all see equally far and there are some of us who cannot distinguish one colour from another. Colour-blind persons cannot serve in the army or navy, nor yet as engine-drivers, guards, or signalmen on railways, for, in these occupations, their inability to distinguish colours might cause disasters.

No doubt this defect of vision is inconvenient; still, it need not debar a man from doing great things. Dalton, the famous chemist, who lived early in the nineteenth century, discovered colour-blindness and was himself colour-blind. No one has done more to advance the science of chemistry than he. He opened up a new world to science, and what he taught led up to the researches which are being carried on in our own day.

Take Care of the Eyelids

Besides the eyeball we must take care of the eyelids. There is a delicate membrane lining the eyelid and continuing over the front of the eye which is rather apt to get inflamed and red; and then the little fold of membrane that we can see at the inner corner of the eyes gets inflamed too. This little fold is very interesting, for it is the dwindled remains of a third eyelid. Birds have this eyelid fully developed, and they can pass it across the surface of the eye.

There are two or three things which can be done to cure sore eyelids. First of all, the patient must have plenty of fresh air; next he must have nourishing food. Then it is a good thing to wring out a bit of boric lint in boiling water and apply it to the eyes. You can buy boric lint at any chemist's for a small sum. Or you may use a bit of rag soaked in boiling water that has a little boracic acid powder dissolved in it. You should be very careful about any rags or towels used for this purpose, since sore eyes are contagious.

Structure of the Human Ear

We must now go on to the ear, and I believe you will find its structure no less wonderful than that of the eye.

It is with the ear as with the eye—that which hears is not the ear itself, but the centre in the brain, to which the nerve of hearing, the **auditory nerve**, communicates vibrations received in the ear. And just as the waves of light have to reach the retina before they can make the image, so the waves or vibrations of sound have to reach nerve-endings within the ear before the sensation of sound can be aroused.

Our ear consists of three parts, the outer, the middle, and the inner ear, besides the external flap which we see by the side of the head. The three parts are separated from one another by delicate stretched membranes, and the nerve-endings are in the inner ear. We will look at this first, for it is the most important of the three chambers.

You will see by the diagram that faces page 114 that this inner or true ear itself consists of two parts. Above is an arrangement of three loop-like figures; below, a twisted object much like a snail's shell. Both are hollow tubes filled with fluid. The first are the **semi-circular canals**. These have nothing to do with hearing, but they are very important, for they give us the sense of equilibrium or balance. The second —called the **cochlea** (snail-shell) is the ear proper, the place in which are those nerve-endings that respond as the vibrations strike against them, and send the sound-message along the auditory nerve to the brain.

But how are the vibrations of the air to reach the inner ear and the nerve-endings in the cochlea? They pass through the outer ear and the middle ear.

The outer ear is a winding passage. The sound vibrations pass down it and cause the membrane, or drum of the ear, which closes the end of the passage, to vibrate. These vibrations are then sent on to the middle ear where they are caught up by a chain of three little bones, slung by muscles across the chamber on the inner side of the drum. The curious shape of these little bones may be judged from their names: the hammer, the anvil, and the stirrup. These convey the vibrations to the membrane at the entrance of the inner or true ear, and thence to the fluid and the nerve-endings.

There is a passage which leads from the middle ear into the throat. Thus you will understand that one reason why we should never neglect a sore throat is the possibility of harm to the ear from it. It is also very important to remember that breathing through the mouth may lead to deafness, the ear and the mouth being so closely connected.

How the Ear is Protected

The ear is protected by its position in the thickest and strongest bone of the skull. At the same time we must not forget that it is very close to the brain.

The walls of the outer passage leading to the drum contain glands which secrete wax. This wax should only be removed when visible externally, unless by a doctor's orders.

Our ears should be left for the most part to take care of themselves. The only thing that is necessary is to keep the outside part clean.

Never poke about in your ear. Even to get out superfluous wax you should proceed gently, using a bit of soft rag twisted up, not anything hard, because of the delicate membrane at the end of the passage, which once injured cannot be repaired.

Striking on the ear is very dangerous, for it may injure not only the drum, but also the brain, and has been known to cause death. I need hardly say that it is also dangerous to put things in the ear. We saw that a glaring light injures our sight by fatiguing the delicate cells of the retina. We can, however, close our eyes and thus shut out any excess of light. Unfortunately we cannot similarly close our ears to noise which injures the ear, the auditory nerve, and the brain. **Loud noise, especially at night**, exhausts the nerves and brain, and may produce nerve disease. You should therefore remember that to make unnecessary noise—such as whistling, shouting, screaming, banging doors, etc.—is injurious both to yourself and to your neighbours.

Resemblance between the Senses
of Taste and Smell

The senses of taste and of smell resemble one another very closely, as you may have seen in the short account I gave you of their origin. The nerve-endings which enable us to smell are situated in the upper part of the nose. They are grouped together in a part of the passage which is not—as the rest is—covered with cilia. These nerve-endings perceive extremely minute particles of different substances floating in the atmosphere, and report of them to the centre of smell in the brain.

When we wish to smell anything we commonly sniff a little. This is because those minute particles of matter which excite the sense of smell have to be brought into sharp and fresh contact with the nerve-endings, or the smell will not be so well perceived.

The nerve-endings which give us the sense of taste are, as you know, situated in the skin of the tongue; the chief ones are collected together at the back of the tongue within a row of projections called the taste-papillæ (Figure 27).

If you looked through the microscope at a section of one of these taste-papillæ, you would see, in the skin of the sides, little flask-shaped bodies, which are known as taste-buds. They are formed of cells from the skin of the tongue, and into them the nerve-endings run up.

It is a remarkable thing that every substance has to be dissolved before it can be tasted, for the taste-buds

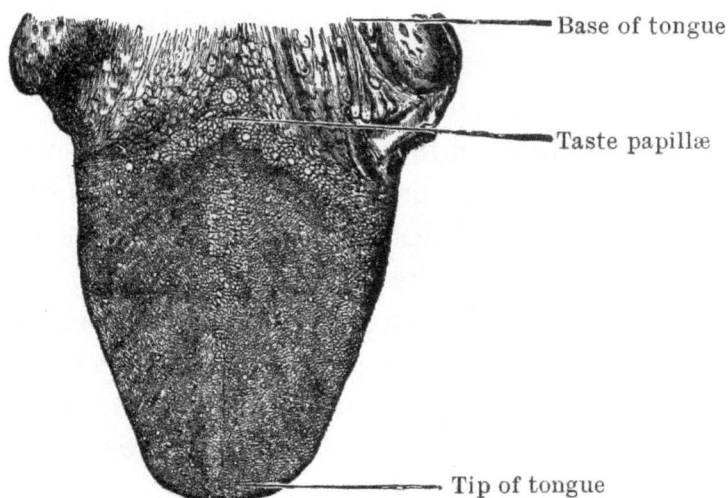

Base of tongue

Taste papillæ

Tip of tongue

FIGURE 27 — THE TONGUE

can only be excited by a substance that is fluid. So if you put anything hard into your mouth you cannot actually taste it till the saliva has dissolved away some part of its surface.

Importance of Training the Senses

We ought to take great pains to train our senses. The quicker and the more accurate they are, the more successful shall we be in all we do with our hands, and the more prompt will become the working of our minds.

Quickness and accuracy of eye and ear are much more valuable to a man than even bodily agility and strength; nay, strength itself depends on these for guidance.

You will find it very interesting in your history, as

well as in the daily life of people around you, to look out for instances of this, and see where a good and quick eye or ear proved to be of the greatest use. We must reckon in this not merely examples of marksmanship of various kinds; nor merely such examples of quick hearing as that of the barbarian who lays his ear to the ground and hears the vibration of horse-hoofs miles away. Besides these we must count in quickness of observation concerning the things of everyday life— readiness in seeing what those around us need; skill in arts and handicrafts, which depends upon the eye; or in music, which depends upon the ear.

Scarcely less important is the sense of touch residing in our fingers. What a blessing skilful hands are! They make the greatest possible difference to everything we do. There are many kinds of work which cannot be even attempted without a quick and well-trained sense of touch—such, for instance, as the work of a surgeon, or that of a maker of delicate instruments.

But, putting such instances aside, skill, or the lack of it, enters into the success or failure of nearly every common action.

And here I should like to remind my girl readers what a beautiful field for the acquiring and the use of skill is afforded by household work. It makes all the difference whose hands prepared the food, made the bed, set the room in order, dressed the child, tended the sick. What comfort, order, and wholesomeness when one person does all this—and perhaps, when another has to do it, what untidiness, muddle, and general discomfort!

Now, there is no doubt that some people are born cleverer with their hands than others; but I can assure you the difference in skill which we see in the world is far more owing to the different degrees of training than to original difference in the muscles and nerves themselves. As for the secret of successful training of all the senses, it is, Begin early.

Sense of Smell

I think we most of us realize, more or less, that the training of eye, ear, and hand is important; but there is one sense, which ought to be of great use to us, which we very much neglect. I am sure our friend the dog, if he could express his opinion, would tell us this neglect is strangely foolish. This sense is that of smell.

Now, we can train our noses to like good smells and to object to bad ones as well as we can train our ears to hear notes in tune. Unfortunately, many people have trained their noses in just the wrong way, so that they are like some girls whom I once used to meet in a club. One evening I went in to their club-room and found it very stuffy. "It is rather close in here," I said. "Oh, yes!" they all cried, "isn't it nice? We do like it. It smells so homey.'"

Now, that showed that in their homes they had trained their sense of smell to like very unwholesome air, charged with carbon dioxide, and with all sorts of particles from the persons and the furniture, and other things in the house and I am afraid that they are by no means the only people who commit this mistake.

We should train our noses first and foremost to like fresh air. Then they will at once detect any unwholesome sort of smell, will dislike it very much, and leave us no peace till we have discovered where it comes from and removed the cause of it. There is no need for stuffiness; the reason of its existence is merely that a majority of people still do not particularly dislike it, or do not notice it.

Alcohol and the Senses

No one who wishes to have keen senses will take alcohol. It spoils the sensitiveness of the nerve-endings; it makes the nerves from each sense-organ slower in conveying the messages to the brain; and it injures the brain itself, so that the messages, when they reach the centres, are received and recorded confusedly instead of clearly.

A healthy man who habitually takes alcohol has thus less command of his senses than he ought to have, and can place no full dependence upon their report.

The Senses and Memory

One thing more:—All the kinds of knowledge which our senses gather for us and transmit to the brain are stored up there as memories.

How shall we store our memories with good and

beautiful things? There are many treasure-houses from which we may draw, but there is one, the most vast and richest of all, that yields us yet more than the rest. I mean the treasure-house of Nature. Let your eyes and ears be often busy searching there.

CHAPTER VIII

THE BRAIN AND NERVOUS SYSTEM

"What is my ruling faculty now to me?
And of what nature am I now making it?
And for what purpose am I now using it?"

— MARCUS AURELIUS

BEFORE you begin this chapter I should like you to look once more at page 8, where you will find a short account of those cells in an animal's body which have taken upon themselves the work of attending to the world outside and of governing the movements of the animal.

Now we have seen that all the different parts and organs of the human body are the counterpart of similar parts and organs in the bodies of animals. This is more especially the case when we compare man with the mammals or highest vertebrates; yet it holds true throughout most of the animal kingdom, and the more you know about man on the one hand, and his brother animals on the other, the deeper you will find this correspondence goes.

Suppose you were asked what it is which makes the

132

difference between men and animals, I wonder what you would answer. Perhaps some of you would say, Man walks upright. True, but so to a certain extent do some of the larger apes—though they also walk on all fours, which we cannot manage very well. Then another may say, Men live in cities; they till the ground, invent machines, and speak. This answer is more nearly the right one. It is true that anyone, who observes ants and bees, and reads what others have discovered about them, may see that they also live in cities after their fashion, that they have laws and division of labour, and even, in the case of some of the ants, till the ground in their own way.

Yet, great as must be the admiration we feel for the cleverness of ants and bees, their cities and inventions are not to be compared with those of man and it is **in the brain**, the organ which enables man to observe the outside world, and to reflect and act upon what he observes, that we find the one immense superiority of man over the other living creatures of the world.

That part of the brain, of which I have spoken several times in the preceding chapters, which governs the thoughts, the senses, and the actions they choose to perform, fills but a small space in the front of the skull of many vertebrate animals. In the more intelligent, it is generally found to be larger relatively than in the less intelligent, as we might expect. In man it stretches backward from the forehead in two great lobes which fill the whole arch of the skull.

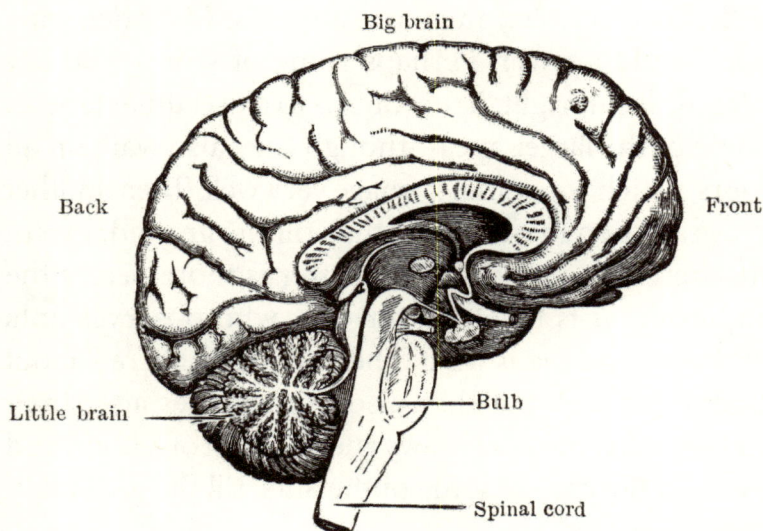

Big brain

Back

Front

Little brain

Bulb

Spinal cord

FIGURE 28 — BRAIN CUT LENGTHWISE

The Brain and its Work

We will call this the **big brain** (Figure 28). At the back of it, continuous with it and somewhat underneath it, is the **little brain**; behind and under that we have the **bulb**, and then the **spinal cord**, which goes down the whole length of the backbone through the channel formed in the vertebræ of which I told you in another chapter. The **little brain**, the **bulb**, and the **spinal cord** are all concerned in that work which goes on within us without our perceiving it.

The brain communicates with every part of the body by means of nerve-threads or fibres, which branch and branch till they become too small to be seen by the naked eye (Figure 29). Their endings are in the skin, in

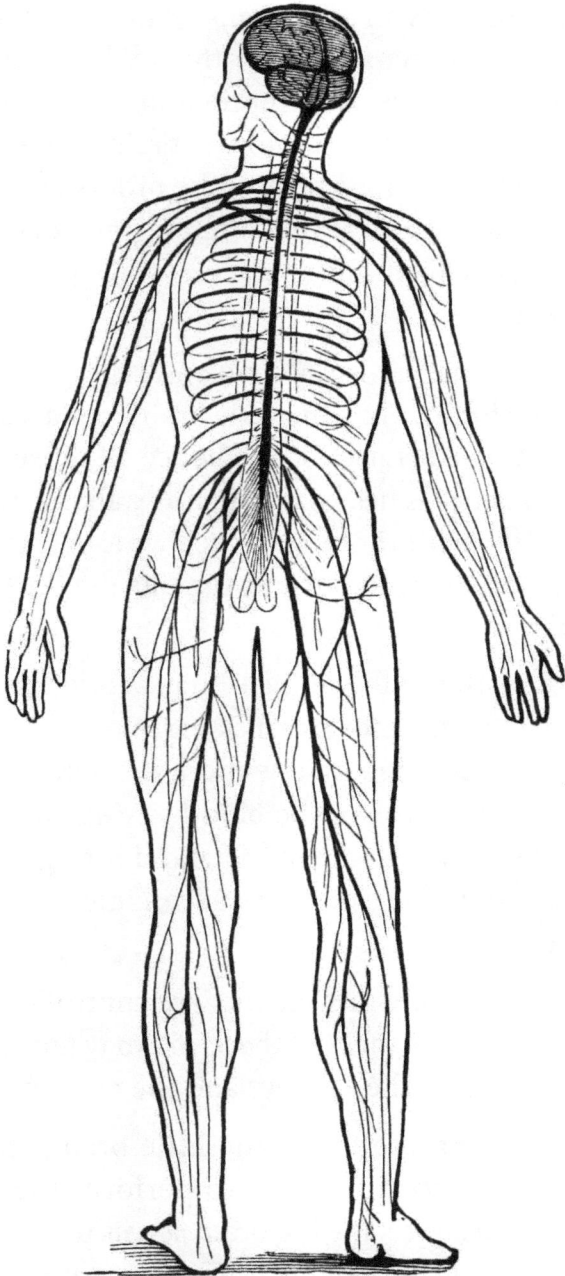

FIGURE 29 — DIAGRAM OF THE NERVOUS SYSTEM

muscles, in glands, in sense-cells—almost everywhere. These nerve-endings and nerve-threads have not all the same work. Some receive impressions from the world outside and send them up to the brain; these are the **sensory** nerves. Others receive the orders of the brain and carry them down to the different parts of the body, and these are called **motor nerves**, since they start all movement.

Different nerves carry their messages to different parts of the brain. Thus the little brain manages the co-ordination of the muscles, and hence all those actions in which balance is necessary, such as walking, running, jumping. If the little brain is injured we topple over, and fall about, while in all our movements the muscles act uncertainly.

Then in the bulb we have that part of the brain which directs such movements as are necessary for life —breathing, secretion, many of the movements of the food-pipe, and those of the blood-vessels. If the bulb is injured you can readily understand how great must be the danger to life, since by such an injury breathing itself may be stopped.

Yet other bodily movements are controlled by the spinal cord. As instances of these you may take the acts of excretion from the kidneys and the rectum.

As long as these three, the little brain, the bulb, and the spinal cord, are able to perform their work without disturbance, the big brain seems to leave them to themselves; but when any difficulty is encountered, or injury suffered, we discover how closely, after all, the big brain is connected with them. The nerves belonging to the part which is damaged then pass on a message to the nerve-fibres which run to the big brain, and we feel pain, great or slight according as the message given is more or less urgent.

The big brain is also able to interfere in some of, though not in all, the work of the rest of the brain. Thus we may choose to hold our breath—the orders from the one part contradicting those from the other part of the brain. But we can only continue to do this for a short time for when the bulb has almost no more oxygen left it sends so vehement an order to the muscles to let go that we are forced to obey, whether we will or not.

Those actions which are performed independently of our knowledge and will have received the name of **reflex actions**. You would find it very interesting to make a list of all the reflex actions you know of. Among them you must reckon such actions as blinking the eyes when dust has got into them, jumping at a sudden prick, or starting at a sudden noise.

Grey Matter

The structure of the brain is, as you may imagine, exceedingly complicated, and is too difficult to be explained here. If we examine a fresh brain—that of a sheep, for instance we can see with the naked eye that it is composed of two kinds of matter, one grey, the other white.

The grey matter lies on the surface, arranged, as you

may see in the diagram, in many folds. It is the most active part of the brain. It receives all the messages of sensation—sight, hearing, pleasure, pain, whatever they may be. It starts those impulses which speed back to gland or muscle, and cause all the movements that take place in the body. It is also the organ of our memory, of our will, of our reason and emotion—of all that we mean when we speak of the mind of a man.

The brain records within itself every message it has ever received. No sight or sound, nothing done or suffered or thought, can be wiped out of that record. Many things may not have been understood at the time, many others may have been apparently long forgotten; but the record of the impression, as the grey matter of the brain received it, is still there. More than that, some unusual circumstance may call into activity those particular cells of the brain which had stored up the forgotten, half-understood sight or event—and then the impression made will be revealed. A well-known story will show you what I mean.

There was once, in Germany I believe, a village girl who was the servant of a clergyman. Her master was very learned in Hebrew, and he had a habit of walking up and down a part of the garden within earshot of the kitchen, and reciting portions of the Bible in Hebrew. The girl heard him, but, of course, did not pay any attention nor understand what the sounds meant, and she could not have repeated them in her ordinary state. But it happened, some time after she had left the parsonage, that she was taken very ill, and carried to a hospital, and there she amazed all the nurses and doctors by reciting in her delirium long passages from the Hebrew Scriptures. Without her knowing it, or wishing it, her brain had recorded the unknown words she had heard her master utter, and in the disturbance of the brain caused by her illness, the record had, as it were, leapt into activity.

This should show you that we can never say that any sight or sound or event shall make no difference to us. You, who are young, should take care to fill your mind with images and impressions of things that are good and beautiful. For as your brains have not received so many impressions as those of an older person they retain what they receive all the more clearly, and you may easily, if you will, store them with knowledge that will enable you to judge rightly and act wisely later on when you have to act and judge for yourselves more than you do now.

White Matter

The white matter of the brain is that which passes the messages to and fro—messages which, going to the grey matter, produce sensation, and, going from it, produce movement in some part of the body.

Now the more often any message is sent either up or down, the more easily, as a rule, it is conveyed.

Let us take messages sent along the nerve of sight as an instance of the first kind. No doubt you have noticed how little children, and even grown people, stare at things which they see for the first time. A new message-track is being made in the brain, and hence what we feel as attention and effort are aroused. This will be especially the case if some kind of judgment has to be formed. Thus, at first, one may have to look very carefully to see whether a line is straight or not but after some practice one becomes able to see this at a glance. So you may notice among workmen that some have a much better eye than others. This may, indeed, be due to natural gift or defect but is more often owing to the fact that many people leave off the effort of attention too soon, before that particular track, if we may so call it, in the brain has been made clear and definite enough.

Again, a person who has naturally but little ear for tune, may, by attending carefully to the notes he hears, become, by degrees, and after some length of time, able to distinguish the differences between them. The track of hearing in the brain will form a better pathway than before.

It is the same with repetition along the motor nerves which lead to action. See how slowly and laboriously a small child writes, and what an easy thing writing is to the clerk in an office! Or watch the clerk adding up his list of figures—how rapidly he works now! and what toil such sums were when he first began them! How we hammer our fingers in our early attempts at carpentry or how we flounder and gasp when we first try to swim! And then in the end how easily we disport ourselves in the water, and how neatly we use our tools—for the brain and nerves are now so accustomed to control these particular kinds of action that we perform a great part of them without even thinking about it.

Practice makes Perfect

This is the meaning of the law, Practice makes Perfect. It is a law we ought all to bear in mind, but those who are young most of all, and that for two reasons.

In the first place the training of the brain is very much easier, and much more may be accomplished by it, when one is young.

In the second place it holds true both ways. If we persist in doing things badly instead of well, we may find we have trained the brain and the nerves to perform them badly always. More than this, there are actions wrong in themselves, to which we are sometimes tempted: if we commit them again and again we may make them habits—that is to say, actions performed almost without our knowing or desiring it, because the brain and nervous system have been so much accustomed to them.

The Lower Animals

You will be able to think out for yourselves a great number of instances of the working of this law of Practice makes Perfect in your own lives and in what you know of other people. But it may be worth while to turn for a minute or two to the animals, and see whether we can observe anything of the same kind in them. Can they too practise some action, at first unfamiliar, and by degrees learn to perform it easily through their brain and nervous system having become used to it?

Yes, indeed they can; and we may see this any day by watching the habits of domestic animals and the ways in which men train them. The young colt does not understand all at once that a twitch of the bridle on the right side of his mouth means, Turn to the right, and a twitch on the left, Turn to the left. He has to be taught this by many repetitions, running round and round his trainer, now this way and now that. In the end, however, the brain of a well-trained horse responds so readily that he will obey the lightest movement of the reins, and you may drive him with no more than a lift of your fingers. No doubt you have seen horses who have been taken often the same round, to deliver bread, or meat or milk, who come to know the streets and the houses so well that they go from one to another of themselves, and might almost be trusted to go the round alone.

The same kind of thing happens with dogs. You will think of sheep-dogs, retrievers, dogs that take blind men about, dogs that perform tricks.

In Switzerland and Bavaria the cows of a village go up to the pastures on the mountain-side in the summer mornings, and return in the evening to be milked. The owners of the cows open the stable-doors, but they take no further trouble about them for one of the cows is the leader and has a loud bell hung round her neck. As she walks through the village, the other cows hear the bell, and each comes out of her stall and joins the leader as she passes. Then the whole herd makes its way up to the pasture, and remains there till the leader starts home, when the band of cows follows her back to the village, and each, as she passes her own stall, falls out of the procession and goes in.

The tricks performing animals are taught are, of course, in some ways mere amusements, but they have a real value in that they show that the brains of animals resemble ours in kind, and that they are able to learn by means of practice just as we do. Perhaps you will think of this next time you hear a parrot talk, or see animals perform in a circus, or teach your dog a new trick.

The wonderful thing is that this power to learn is found far more widely throughout the animal kingdom than you might at first suppose. You will discover what I mean when you come to read the works of Charles Darwin, as I hope you will later on. He has taught us more about this than anyone had ever done before and his work has been the foundation upon which the men of science of our own day have built up a new and surprising knowledge.

FIGURE 30 — CHARLES DARWIN

He showed, as no one had shown before, that all living things are akin to one another—that all life is one.

He taught us that life arose from very simple and lowly beginnings, and advanced generation after generation till it has come to be what we now see it—so varied and beautiful. But for the present the intelligence of animals, and the habits they are able to acquire, should teach you that the law of Practice makes Perfect is one of the great universal laws of life. If we wish to lead good and useful lives we must be very careful as to what we practise.

Fresh Air and Nourishing Food Necessary for the Brain

It is now time to consider the principal points to be observed in taking a reasonable care of the brain and nervous system.

As a matter of fact, I believe that you would be able to find them all out for yourselves, if you reflected on what you already know, and simply used your commonsense to form a judgment upon it. Still, it may be useful to make a few suggestions here.

We have seen that the brain is a centre of the utmost activity. Activity means expenditure of energy; and it follows, does it not? that where much energy is expended, much must be supplied.

What is the source whence all our energy is drawn? You will answer immediately, The oxygen of the air. Then it is obvious that nothing is more important for the health of the brain than fresh air. Anyone who spends much time in a close or overcrowded room will necessarily grow drowsy, stupid, and incapable of vigorous work or enjoyment. Sometimes strong excitement will keep off these effects for a while, but they are always perceived in the end. Persons who pass most of their lives indoors, and do not constantly renew the air around them from outside, become feeble, not only in body, but also in mind.

Hence the first point to remember is, Have all the fresh air you can;—be out of doors as much as is in any way possible, and, when indoors, see to it that your windows are open, by night as well as by day.

If I wrote pages and pages about the need the brain has of fresh air, I could not exaggerate the importance of it. Still, fresh air is not the only thing necessary; we must have good food as well, for without food we cannot make red blood corpuscles, and, as you know, without the red blood corpuscles the blood cannot carry the oxygen. Moreover, in the brain, as in every other part of the body, there is a certain amount of waste going on, and this has to be made good by nourishment; while, as we learn and observe more and more, the brain-cells undergo changes, and become more and more active, and require nourishment for this also.

So the second piece of advice I would give you is, Eat good and nourishing food; eat enough—but, on the other hand, do not eat too much.

The Brain Needs Exercise

Fresh air and good food will not, however, by themselves, make us quick-witted, thoughtful or well-informed. The brain is made to be used, and it is very bad for it to be idle. No one who has fresh air, sufficient food, and the right intervals of rest need be afraid of overworking it. In fact, men of science who have made a special study of the matter tell us that most people work their brains far too little.

The Germans have a very expressive word, "denkfaul"—think-idle—which they apply to those who will not use their brains. Unfortunately this word would very well describe large numbers of men and women. As you grow older you will see that this failing of indolence of mind, has done almost more to prevent success and happiness than all other failings put together. Among other evils it causes people to become "set in their ways" and incapable of learning.

Now that you know how great an effect habit has upon the brain, more especially in youth, you should take pains to accustom your brain to work thoroughly. This means, Give to everything you do your full attention; never be content till you have got to the bottom of things, and do not be put off by difficulties. At first you may find real brainwork troublesome, but if you go on with it steadily you will end by finding it a source of great delight.

And Rest

So far, we have seen that the brain needs oxygen, food, and exercise; we must further remember that it needs rest. Work as **hard** as ever you can—the harder the better but do not work too **long**. For boys and girls of thirteen or fourteen, half-an-hour at a time is long enough to spend over any kind of learning that is at all difficult; and even in the case of easy subjects, three-quarters of an hour will be rather beyond the limit, unless, indeed, the work is such as employs the hands, or permits of movement at the same time. Little children must, of course, have far shorter lessons than this; ten minutes or a quarter of an hour is enough for them. It is no use making up your mind that you will go on with a certain piece of work till you have finished it; for if the nerve-cells concerned in it are fatigued, they will make errors, and you will find later on that you did badly what you persisted in doing thus unwisely.

Now, there are two ways of resting the brain. The first is, change of occupation, which calls into greater activity nerve-cells that were but slightly occupied before, and leaves those which are fatigued gradually to recover their energy. Thus, for instance, physical exercise, and handiworks such as carving, cookery, and carpentry, are good between sedentary lessons; and a walk or games good after a morning spent over books. A few minutes in the middle of a difficult lesson spent in running, hopping, or breathing exercise— with the windows thrown wide open—will freshen up brains beginning to grow tired. You will also readily understand that nothing refreshes the brain so much as time spent in the open air. As the day goes on, however, the brain and nerves, whether we notice it or not, lose something of their power to work. Hence a wise person so arranges his time that his hardest work comes in the morning, and easy work and recreation towards the end of the day.

This brings us to the second and most important way of resting the brain—

Sleep

In sleep the circulation undergoes a certain amount of change, and less blood is supplied to the brain; thus you will see that rest in sleep has a character of its own, and other kinds of rest cannot take the place of it. A child of four needs fourteen hours' sleep; a child of seven about thirteen hours. At twelve or fourteen we want ten hours' sleep, and not till the age of twenty-one can we do with less than nine, if we wish our brains to be vigorous and to work well. It is a great thing to go to bed early, for the best sleep is before midnight. Few things are worse for those who are still growing than late hours.

Importance of Self-Control

I have one more point to remind you of as important for the well-being of the brain and nervous system and that is the necessity for **self-control**. We are all of us inclined to yield on the one hand to various kinds of passion or excitement, and on the other to laziness and shirking. Either may in time become, by frequent indulgence, a habit; and so we find people who cannot govern their temper or their jealousy, their love of pleasure or their greed, and others who cannot make themselves take trouble about anything, who are listless and foolish, and often poor and miserable, though, if they had trained themselves to be energetic, they need never have been so.

The way to prevent either of these misfortunes is to try steadily to know what is right, and to do it, not flinching if this should happen to be disagreeable. Such conduct trains and strengthens the will, and keeps the brain and nerves active and healthy.

There are some dangers you should be careful to avoid, especially while you are still young and can easily form habits, whether good or bad. I will mention here the two or three which are most common.

First comes the use of alcohol. No part of the body is so susceptible to the influence of alcohol as are the brain and nerves; and its influence is most disastrous. It depresses and weakens them even when taken in small quantities; if taken habitually it cannot fail to make them more and more incapable of action. When used to excess alcohol in time renders the brain practically useless as an organ of thought, and at last may so enfeeble it that it can no longer even govern the most necessary functions of the body.

Secondly comes the smoking of tobacco. This is especially harmful while one is young; it injures the whole nervous system, preventing its proper growth and development. It also prevents the formation of good habits of mind.

And thirdly comes the reading of trash. This is far more injurious than most people seem to think. It is bad for the eyes, since such stuff is commonly ill-printed and read very fast; and it is bad for the mind, since it destroys a taste for better things just when it might be beginning to spring up. It undermines the power of steady attention, and increases that craving for excitement which makes a person impatient of work and eager for pleasure. And then, in the end, one gets weary of the trash, and yet cannot enjoy any better reading. Of course I do not mean that you should never read anything amusing. On the contrary, a good story, a good joke, a hearty laugh are among the best things in the world. But there is plenty of good literature that will supply you with these, and if you are determined to have an active, keen, and happy mind you will keep to the good literature and scorn the trash.

Man's Mind his Greatest Possession

I hope that of the girls and boys who read this book there are none without some special hobby or interest.

No doubt many of my girl readers have thought a good deal about nursing, about the care of little children, about cookery or keeping house, or beautiful needlework, as well as about the different kinds of learning we get from books.

As for my boy readers, there must be many who are enthusiastic about engineering, or carpentry, or gardening; others, perhaps, want to go to sea some day; others love the country and country work; and doubtless there are several who love reading.

Now, if each of you will think of his or her favourite business in life, and consider what is the manner in which great things have been accomplished in it, you will see that for nearly everything a good deal of apparatus, a number of implements, are needed.

The carpenter must have his bench, with the tools belonging to it; the sailor must have his ship, and the farmer his ploughs and harrows. The nurse cannot get on without many appliances, nor the needlewoman without her needles and stuffs and threads; the engineer must have his machines, and the scholar his books.

Now ask yourselves one or two questions about this. Who invented all these different tools and instruments? You will say, Different people at different times. And now, how did they invent them?—The idea came into their minds; they thought of it.

Again, how is it we are able to use all these different inventions? A ship, for instance, may be the best ship ever made, but there must be a man at the wheel before it can fulfil its purpose. Or you may have a fire, and pots and pans, and meat and flour and vegetables, all of the very best, and if you have no one to use them there will be no food prepared. Moreover, if the man at the wheel is half asleep, or the girl who is cooking is lazy and ignorant, the excellence of the ship and the excellence of the food will alike come to nothing.

If you consider this attentively you will see that poor tools or material with good will and intelligence in the person who uses them turn out better work than the best possible tools in the hands of one who is incompetent or careless.

Then it follows—does it not?—that the mind of a man or woman is something more useful and more precious than any instruments or tools ever known, since it is the mind, after all, which both invents and uses such things.

We should think a man foolish who let the machinery of his factory go to rack and ruin because he would not trouble himself about it. Yet such a one is not so foolish as the man who neglects his own mind, or indulges himself in habits which injure it.

If you follow these thoughts out, by a little reflection you will see that it is right and becoming for each one of us to respect his own mind, and to value it as his greatest and best possession. We ought to deem no calamity so great as that of losing our power of thought and judgment, our strength of will and our sincerity of feeling; and no good fortune so much to be desired as that of growing every day more thoughtful, more loyal to what is right, more gentle, more open-minded, and more truly wise.

If we thus respect our own minds we shall no less respect the mind of our neighbour, as having in it the same powers and possibilities.

It is upon these two foundations, respect for oneself and respect for one's neighbour, that the State in its highest form is built up.

CHAPTER IX

BACTERIA

"Perseverance in effort."

— Pasteur's Motto

SOME seventy years ago, if you could have visited what was called the Communal College in the little town of Arbois, in the East of France, you might have seen Louis Pasteur working there as a scholar.

You might have heard from the head of the college that the boy was the son of a tanner, of a poor man, whose life was something of a struggle, yet one who was thoughtful and well-informed, who had served in the Army, and been decorated on the field of battle.

"Louis Pasteur," the principal of the college might have continued, "is just now but a child. He will spend whole days away from work, fishing. He draws portraits—and by no means bad ones—of all his friends, instead of doing his home-lessons. Still, he has great talents, and some day, when he comes to reason, he will do well."

It was not long before Louis Pasteur's reasoning powers developed, and then he gave up his childish pursuits and set to work in earnest. What first roused him to energy was his own good heart. He began to understand what sacrifices his father was making in order to give him a good education, and to realize what hopes he would disappoint if he neglected his opportunities.

So he threw himself into his work with a will, and the habit of industry, once formed, never left him. It was the beginning of a life of great success and great fame, for his work has benefited all mankind, and his name is known and honoured all over the world.

New Work for Pasteur

Louis Pasteur worked at chemistry, and made several most brilliant discoveries in that science. He had been in Paris for some years, and was in the full current of ideas, observations, and experiments, when he was entreated to give all this up and undertake work of quite a new kind.

The entreaty came from a man who had once been Pasteur's master in chemistry, for whom he had an affectionate and grateful regard. If it had not been for this he would have refused to give up what he was so eagerly engaged upon, especially as he knew nothing about the subject of the research, and, moreover, would be obliged to leave Paris, and go to the far South of France.

However, in the end he yielded to the wishes of his old master.

The people in the South of France, as no doubt you have read in your geography, depend on the silk industry; and the silk industry, of course, depends on the silkworm.

I daresay most of you have kept silkworms in some little box, or in the corner of a drawer. You have fed them on lettuce leaves,

FIGURE 31 — LOUIS PASTEUR

instead of the mulberry leaves which are their ordinary food, and have watched all their changes—from the egg to the "worm"; then from the "worm," through its four moultings, to the chrysalis in its lovely yellow cocoon and from the chrysalis to the moth. You know, of course, that silkworms are not really worms, but are a kind of caterpillar, though for the sake of convenience we will here use the popular name.

These changes are watched most anxiously by thousands in the South of France, and in the year 1849 there was great dismay in the country, for a disease attacked the silkworms and killed enormous numbers of them before they had even begun to spin their cocoons. It spread from one batch of worms to another, and the silk crop was a failure.

The following years were little or no better.

Summer after summer the cultivators tried every-thing they could think of, but until 1865 they had had only one good year since the disease broke out; and meanwhile the trouble had spread into all the silk-growing countries except Japan.

Many people were ruined; everyone who had anything to do with silk was in despair and a great petition was presented to the Government begging that scientific men might be sent from Paris to search out the cause of the plague and the means to stop it.

The Government communicated with Pasteur's old master, asking for his advice, and he, as I told you, urged that Pasteur should undertake the investigation.

He Discovers the Cause of the Silkworm Disease

When Pasteur arrived at Alais, where the research was to be carried on, and saw the misery of the town and all the neighbourhood, he ceased to regret the beloved work he had given up—his one desire was to help these poor people.

He had not been more than a few hours in Alais before he had examined a number of silkworms under the microscope.

He saw, what one or two other investigators had already seen, that in some of them there were a number of exceedingly minute living bodies or organisms. No one had hitherto paid much attention to these; but it at once occurred to Pasteur that they were probably the cause of the plague.

All that summer, and for two years afterwards, Pasteur laboured unceasingly, helped by his wife and daughter, together with several men who had shared his former work at Paris. The more experiments he made, the clearer it became that those tiny living bodies within the body of the worm were doing all the mischief. They were **parasites**, that is to say, creatures which, instead of getting their own living for themselves, subsist upon the living body of some other creature.

Pasteur found them not in the worms only, but also in the eggs, the chrysalides, and the moths. They multiplied with extreme rapidity, usually appearing first in the intestine, and making their poor victims unable to digest food. From the intestines they would then make their way into the rest of the tissues of the worm, until at length the whole body was so much injured by them that it died.

Sometimes a worm which had escaped the parasites in its earliest days, but had been infected with them later on, would live to spin its cocoon, and even to creep out as a moth and lay its eggs. But such a moth was always very feeble and miserable, and the eggs it laid were found to contain the parasite, which either prevented them from hatching out, or, if the worms were hatched, soon destroyed them.

And How the Disease was Spread

Having discovered what the disease was in itself, Pasteur had to find out how it was spread.

The first means of its spreading was found to be the droppings or **excreta** of the worms, as they crawled upon the mulberry-leaves supplied to them for food. The excreta from an infected worm were found to be full of the parasites, which, being thus thrown out, were often eaten by other worms as they browsed on the leaves.

Another means of contagion was this. Silkworms, as you know if you have kept them, have sharp hooks at the end of their forefeet, and with these, as they crawl about over and under one another, they often prick each other through the skin. Now if the forefeet were besmeared with excreta containing parasites, some of these parasites would be left in the wound made by the prick and thus infect the wounded worm. Again, if a worm pricked one which had contracted the plague, it would almost certainly carry away a number of the parasites upon its claws, and next time it pricked a fellow-worm would introduce the disease into its body.

Yet again, the parasites in the excreta, or in dead worms, were often whirled up in dust when the breeding-houses were being swept. This dust settled down on leaves and worms which perhaps had till then been free from them—sometimes bringing the contagion on the wind to a considerable distance.

All this was found out by means of hard work with the microscope, and by the most carefully-conducted and oft-repeated experiments. At first the whole thing was ridiculed, and Pasteur received letters full of scorn and sometimes of anger, from men of science and persons interested in the silk trade. But he was not a man to give up anything he saw to be true because people opposed him, and did not at first understand him. He worked on steadily, and by-and-by proved beyond the possibility of doubt that his conclusions were right.

The Remedy

And now you will ask what remedy he prescribed for the mischief.

He found, first of all, that the parasites shed from the bodies of worms, or contained in dead worms, did not live till the following summer. After several weeks had passed there was no more danger from them.

The danger lay in those parasites which were hidden in the eggs, which would be in the silkworms when they hatched out, and start the whole thing over again in the next year. Pasteur devised a simple but ingenious method for discovering the eggs which were infected, and destroying them.

When the time came for laying the eggs each moth was placed separately upon a small linen cloth, hung up horizontally. When she had laid her eggs upon it she was fastened to the cloth. As you know, the moths die almost immediately after laying—it was then easy to examine the dead moths one by one with a microscope, and see if any contained parasites. If any were found, the moth, all the eggs she had laid, and the little cloth upon which she had laid them, were promptly burnt, and thus all chance of disease removed.

The cultivators of silkworms no longer fear the plague that had harassed and impoverished them for seventeen years; Pasteur's discovery has ensured them against any return of it, so long as they will take the precautions which he taught them.

Other Diseases Found to be Due to Parasites

Now, the discovery that an infectious disease is caused by a parasite was an extremely great discovery.

One or two men of science had vaguely guessed at it before, but until Pasteur made his experiments on silk-worms nothing of the kind had ever been clearly worked out—still less been put to any practical use.

It was a new light, and a new hope in the world. For you can imagine that Pasteur and the men he had trained to work with him did not stop at the silkworms, but resolved to find out whether any of the diseases which attack other animals and ourselves might not be due to a cause of the same kind.

As soon as he was able to do so Pasteur gave himself most eagerly to this research. By means of those careful observations and experiments which were the great feature in all his work, he brought to light what he expected, viz., that many diseases, both in men and in animals, are caused by parasites, which get into the body with the food eaten, with the air breathed, or perhaps through a cut or a scratch.

He was like a pioneer advancing into a new country, hewing out paths as he went; and a great army of men of science has followed, is still following, in his steps.

They have shown, as clearly as Pasteur showed it in the case of the silkworms, that by far the greater number of the illnesses we hear of are due to parasites.

These parasites are for the most part tiny plants, each consisting of only one cell. Many are in the shape of minute rods; hence they are called **bacteria**, the Greek word for rods. Certain kinds are also called **bacilli**, the same thing in Latin; while the word **microbe**—meaning tiny living thing—is used also as a name for them.

Smallness and Rapid Multiplication of Bacteria

It is difficult to give you an idea of the minuteness of these bacteria. Some are rather larger than others; but it would take 20,000 of a good-sized sort, placed in a row side by side, to reach the length of an inch. Or we may put it in another way, and say that one square inch is room enough for 400 millions of them, in a single layer.

So pray do not imagine, as some people have done before now, that you could see bacteria flying or crawling about. One must look through a microscope lens of considerable power to be able to see them even as specks.

Another thing we must bear in mind is that not all bacteria are harmful. On the contrary, many of them are so useful that the life of the world would hardly get on without them. But this chapter will become too long if I try to tell you about these, and so here we will consider chiefly those which may be called our particular enemies.

If you ask me where bacteria are to be found, the safest answer would seem to be, Everywhere. They are in the air; in food of all kinds; in our own mouths and intestines, and in those of animals; on our skin and hair, and under our nails; on our walls and floors and ceilings, and furniture and clothing; in the farmyard, in the street; in water, in the soil; and, more especially, in all kinds of dust. In fact, it is more difficult to say where they are not than where they are. In the air on the top of high mountains, and out on mid-ocean, they are hardly found, but it may be taken for granted that they are everywhere else, sometimes in greater, sometimes in smaller numbers; some of them, as I said, harmless, some very useful, and some very deadly.

You will see in the accompanying plate the form of some of them. For purposes of experiment many kinds have been cultivated by placing a few of them in a liquid or prepared jelly which suits them as food. It is then discovered that some of them possess the most beautiful colours, bright scarlet, bright yellow, green, brown, purple, and black, etc.

A yet more important discovery made by this means is that of their rapid multiplication. Each little plant divides into two, and these into two again, and so on; and, under favourable conditions, this is done so quickly that from a single cell you may have, at the end of one day, 16,800,000 bacteria.

It is the multiplication of these tiny living things in the blood or the tissues of an animal which forms the beginning of an infectious disease.

Diseases caused by Bacteria

What diseases in man are caused by bacteria? I will give you a list of the most common ones:—

Cholera.	Influenza.
Consumption.	Pneumonia.
Diphtheria.	Typhoid fever.
Rheumatism.	

And almost certainly also the following:—

Catarrh (common cold).	Measles.
	Mumps.
Chicken-pox.	Scarlet-fever.
Dysentery.	Whooping-cough.

The bacteria which cause these diseases have been found in perfectly healthy persons. They are lying in wait, so to say, within our bodies, or upon our skin, till they get their chance to multiply. And their chance is given them whenever we are weakened by any cause

—such as chill, fatigue, lack of fresh air, of sunlight, of proper nourishment, or indulgence in alcohol.

The weaker a person is the more severely he is likely to have any disease. Alcohol weakens the body, and therefore those who take it freely are at a serious disadvantage.

The terrible disease of **small-pox** is caused by a minute body which is not a plant, but an animal.

We must not mention small-pox without pausing for one moment to recollect what ravages it once caused. A hundred years ago very great numbers of people died of it, and a very large proportion of the population of Europe was 'pock-marked,' showing how common was the disease. A face marked with small-pox is rarely seen nowadays.

Our deliverance from this truly awful scourge is due to the introduction of vaccination. You will find it very interesting to look up the history of vaccination in the lives of Lady Mary Wortley Montagu and Dr. Edward Jenner, both of whom lived during the eighteenth century.

It is only necessary here to say what a grievous pity it is that so many persons, who are not very well informed, set themselves against having their children vaccinated. They are exposing them to one of the most dreadful diseases known to humanity, and doing what lies in their power to prevent its being stamped out altogether.

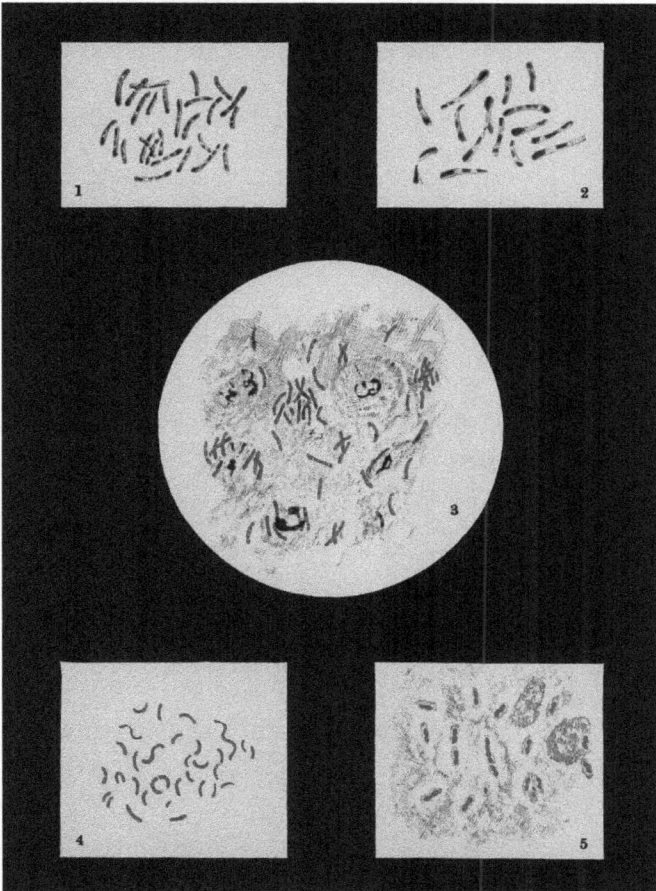

PLATE IV — WHAT BACTERIA LOOK LIKE
WHEN STAINED AND GREATLY MAGNIFIED

1. Microbe which causes diphtheria, after one day's growth, seen as blue rods.
2. The same after five days' growth.
3. Microbe which causes consumption, seen as red rods.
4. Microbe which causes cholera, seen as red rods.
5. Microbe which causes pneumonia, seen as red rods in lung tissue stained pink.

How to Avoid Diseases

Now when it is found that a disease is caused by bacteria two things may be regarded as certain:

First, that it is preventible, being due to dirt of some sort—though, of course, it may not be the fault of the sufferer himself.

Secondly, that it can spread from one person to another.

This book is not meant to show you how to deal with diseases, so I will not go into the question of how the different kinds of bacteria are spread, nor yet of how long each kind may remain in the body of a person before it has multiplied to such an extent that he becomes ill.

Only you should remember that in many, if not in all, of the diseases caused by them, the sick person breathes them out into the air, while anything that comes from his body, or that touches his body, will in most cases be full of them. That is why anyone ill with a disease caused by bacteria should be isolated, or kept apart, as is now required by law for the more serious kinds and now that you understand why this is done I hope you will never resist or complain about such isolation, either for yourself or for anyone else.

About Colds

Many people do not realize that the little ailment usually called a "cold" is caused by bacteria; they think it comes from sitting in a draught, getting one's feet wet, or things like that. Such cannot possibly of themselves give one a "cold"; they only appear to do so because the chilling of the body makes it temporarily weaker, and so gives any bacteria that may have found their way in a chance to get the upper hand. As the bacteria of "cold" are very common, especially in towns, we cannot help often breathing them in; thus it is no wonder we sometimes get colds. In Nansen's expedition to the far North no one ever caught one. It was only when the explorers returned home, and once more breathed the air of towns and the bacteria, that colds troubled them.

Whenever you have a cold remember you are infectious, and out of consideration for other people, take sensible measures to stop it, and keep apart as much as possible till it is gone.

Never use an apron or shirt-sleeve for wiping the nose, but use a pocket-handkerchief or some soft old rag for the purpose, and also when coughing or sneezing.

Another Point

This brings me to another point of which we should be mindful. Some bacteria—such as those of which we have just been speaking—may do comparatively little harm to one person, and a great deal of harm to another if they are handed on to him. The degree of harm depends on the constitution and the strength of each individual. So we must not be careless about the infection of what seem unimportant kinds of illness, such as whooping-cough, mumps, or chicken-pox. If some children take them but slightly it does not follow that the next boy or girl to whom they may be handed on will be equally fortunate. Many children have been made weak and ailing for years from the effects of what is generally reckoned an unimportant illness. Moreover even a very slight attack of any kind of illness leaves some mark or tendency to weakness behind it, though we may not notice it.

How we are Guarded against Bacteria

When first people learnt about the existence of bacteria they were considerably alarmed; and perhaps from what I have told you, some of you have begun to feel that if these bacteria are so numerous, and multiply so fast, there is no chance of conquering them, and almost no use in attempting to fight them.

Not a bit of it! I told you from the first that when any disease had been traced to bacteria it might be considered preventible. To keep them down, two things are necessary: first, to know what to do; secondly, to do it.

In the first place you must remember that our own bodies fight for us, and if we only give them a proper chance, they may he trusted to fight for the most part successfully. The best of all securities against bacteria is good, sound, vigorous health, such as is to be got by eating good food, breathing pure air, taking the right amount of exercise and of rest, and, I may also add, doing the right amount of determined work. If it is bad to be overworked, it is equally bad to be underworked.

The more vigorous is the health of any nation, the less we find among them bacteria, and the diseases caused by bacteria. A very good instance of this is furnished by the Japanese, who, as a nation, know what are the laws of health, and follow them, and are thus much more healthy than we are. We have only to follow these laws in the same way, and we shall assuredly, in a little time, see similar results; and I hope that all the boys and girls now growing towards manhood and womanhood will determine to do all in their power towards bringing this about.

In the second place, the bacteria of disease have a great enemy, whom we should take for our great ally— no less an enemy than the sun himself. Most of them like dark, damp places to flourish in, and when the sunlight falls on them they languish and die.

So remember to let the sunlight into your house. Do not live in a sunless room if you can avoid it; and, in a sunny one, do not be for ever drawing down your blinds the moment the sunshine comes in. It is a pity to think too much of furniture. Better faded colours on your wall-paper than on your own cheeks. If the "body is more than raiment," surely it is also more than carpets and curtains.

What I am telling you has been proved true by most careful experiments which I cannot stop to recount, but I must tell you that it was proved by the same experiments that the sunlight was made even more effective in destroying bacteria, if the oxygen of the air was allowed to reach them at the same time. So while your rooms and your clothes are being sunned, let them be aired too. Have your windows open all you can, the more the better. In time you will grow as hardy as the Japanese, who live in paper houses, and let the winter winds whistle through them day and night without minding it in the least.

Consumption

If we let sunlight and air into our houses, we shall be doing the best thing possible to keep off from us and those dear to us, what has been called in America the great white plague. I mean, consumption, that terrible disease which destroys 40,000 lives in Great Britain every year—young lives, for the most part.

Consumption is a preventible disease, caused chiefly by dirty surroundings. The bacillus of consumption was discovered some years ago by a German, Professor Robert Koch, one of the greatest men who have followed in Pasteur's track.

Since the discovery more and more has been found out about the conditions which will destroy the bacillus on the one hand, or foster it on the other. Every day it becomes clearer that consumption is so rife among us because we are not clean enough, because we do not love sunlight and air enough. If everyone would hate all darkness, stuffiness, and dirt, and would banish them from the place he lived in, this scourge would in quite a short time be done away.

The means by which consumption is most often spread is spitting. What a consumptive person has spat out upon the ground dries up; the bacteria in it are caught in the air; as they float about they are breathed in by other people, and those persons who are too weak to resist them become consumptive.

It may also happen that a man who is not himself consumptive may have these bacilli in his mouth, and cast them forth when he spits and what did no harm to him may do great harm to some other who breathes it in.

A consumptive person, or even anyone who has an ordinary cough, should cough or spit into rag or paper, which may be promptly burnt—or else into some vessel full of water and with a disinfectant in it which will prevent the bacteria from being set free into the air. Such a vessel should be emptied down a closet drain.

No self-respecting boy or man should allow himself to spit. The habit is not only in itself most filthy and disgusting, but when we consider the possible consequences to others we can only call it exceedingly selfish and cruel. For you must remember that everything spat from the mouth contains bacteria of some kind.

There is another common habit which is hardly less disgusting and dangerous; I mean that of licking the forefinger when turning over papers or the leaves of a book. In shops one may often see a person lick his forefinger, take up a piece of paper, and then wrap a loaf or cake or some other article of food in it, and

171

hand it to a customer. Anyone who has good taste and cares about cleanliness cannot help considering this extremely unpleasant; but you can now understand that its unpleasantness is not the worst thing about it. This habit is, in fact, one of those which must necessarily help to spread disease, and the sooner everyone leaves it off the better. I hope that no boy or girl who reads this book will ever turn a page of it with a licked forefinger.

Pure Air

Bodily health, sunlight, air—these will give us most powerful aid against bacteria; but yet these may prove too little if we do not also practise cleanliness.

If you recollect by what ways the bacteria gain an entrance into the body you will see how important cleanliness is.

We said that they are breathed in with the air.

It follows, then, that we should breathe clean air. For ordinary practical purposes this means that we should keep our houses (including walls, floors, ceilings and windows), our furniture, our clothing, and our own persons free from dust and dirt—seeing that dust and dirt are the favourite lurking-places of bacteria.

Now many people, who intend to have everything about them very clean, yet make two mistakes. First, they have in their rooms carpets which cover the whole floor and are nailed tight down, so that they can only be taken up once a year or so, and meanwhile collect enormous quantities of dust and bacteria, which are floated into the air whenever there is movement in the room. Besides this they often have large and heavy pieces of furniture, which cannot be readily moved, so that behind and under them there are sure to be nests of dust.

The second mistake is that of sweeping dry dust with a dry broom. This sends all the bacteria floating in the air more than ever; they settle on the clothes, the skin the hair of the people in the house; and they cannot fail to be breathed into their lungs. If they drift out of the window with the dust the same mischief happens to people in the street.

The sensible rule is, Have your carpets and your furniture of such a size and so arranged that a woman can move them without much difficulty and when you are cleaning **take up the dust with a damp cloth.** Your room will be all the sweeter if you use Jeyes' fluid for this. Shake up a teaspoonful of the fluid in a quart bottle full of tepid water, and pour a good cupful of the mixture into the bucketful of water in which you wring out your cloth.

The gain of such cleanliness is double: it does away with the bacteria, and it helps to keep all the people in a house strong and vigorous; for the freshness and cheerfulness of a really clean house are great promoters of good health.

You should be exceedingly careful not to have the air in your house tainted by any smell from sinks or drains. If you ever notice any such smell, do not rest till you have discovered the cause and removed it; for these parts of a house are most apt of all to harbour very harmful bacteria.

Cleanliness of Food

If we are careful about the cleanliness of the air we must be no less careful about the cleanliness of our food. In this there are three points to be remembered.

First, the food itself must be free from bacteria. Fortunately for us, the heat required for cooking destroys them, so that if we are careful about how we keep our cooked food we are safe. And here I must tell you that when meat "turns off," as we say, when milk turns sour, when anything "goes bad," it is again the work of bacteria. In by far the greater number of cases these bacteria, though different from those of ordinary disease, are exceedingly bad for us if we take them in with our food. Butter, milk, and water are the three commonest conveyers of bacteria. We should **boil all our milk, as well as the water we use for drinking**; while butter should be kept in a cool place, and closely covered up.

Secondly, our pots, pans, dishes, plates, and everything else that comes into contact with our food, especially our hands and nails, should be kept clean, for bacteria may be transferred from these to food which in itself is perfectly good, and so enter the food-pipe and set up some illness.

Above all, if we are looking after a baby who is fed from a bottle we must take the greatest care to have the bottle and the rubber nipple perfectly clean.

This is best ensured by boiling the bottle and nipple, which can be done by putting them into cold water and gradually bringing it to the boiling point. Here we may mention that a "Baby's Comforter," or rubber nipple to suck, is dirty, swarms with bacteria, and is very dangerous to use.

Thirdly, we should be careful to protect all our food from flies. Flies very often settle upon substances which are decaying and which swarm with harmful bacteria, and then carry these bacteria to the next object they alight on. This is one of the commonest means by which diseases are conveyed.

Cuts and Wounds

The third way in which disease bacteria find an entrance into the body is through cuts and wounds. This is now the easiest of all to guard against, though not long ago the difficulty was great and terrible.

In the days before Pasteur's discovery very awful suffering was often caused by the inflammation of cuts and wounds, for nearly every wound festered before it healed, and in some cases wounds did not heal at all. Pasteur discovered not only that bacteria caused the festering, but also what substances would keep them off till the wound was healed. One of these is **boracic acid**, as perhaps you know.

When once the discovery of these substances was made, a great English surgeon, Joseph Lister, now Lord

Lister, took it up, and invented methods of using them in the treatment and dressing of wounds. Such methods are now used everywhere, and by every surgeon among civilised people, and it is found that wounds which once would have taken many weeks and even months to heal, will heal in a few days, and with comparatively little pain.

Thus you will understand that Lord Lister must be accounted not only the greatest of the followers of Pasteur, but also one of the greatest benefactors to humanity the world has ever seen.

FIGURE 32 — LORD LISTER

You should be careful not to let any cut get dirt into it, and more especially dirt from field or garden soil; for in such soil, as well as in the dust of streets, are found the bacteria which cause blood-poisoning, abscesses, and lockjaw.

The best thing to do for a small cut is to wash it in warm water that has boracic powder dissolved in it, and then to wrap a bit of boric lint round it.

Bacteria in the Mouth

In the chapter on the Food-pipe I told you about the importance of taking care of the teeth, and now you can understand more fully why this is so necessary.

Decay in teeth is caused by bacteria. These are breathed out by a person whose teeth are attacked by them, and may be breathed in by others, to their great hurt. They are also frequently conveyed in food. If swallowed, these bacteria may cause serious internal diseases.

The same thing applies to the throat. Many people suffer constantly from a slight sore throat, which is caused by bacteria breathed in with the air or swallowed with food. A sore throat is bad both for oneself and for one's neighbours, and should not be neglected. Moreover, bacteria harboured thus in the mouth make the breath disagreeable, and the air around unwholesome.

So read over again the advice given you in the Food-pipe chapter, and put it into practice.

CHAPTER X

HABITS

"Never do anything just because other people do it. Let your touchstone be not, 'Is it usual?' but 'Is it best?'"

— ALMOND

WE have all of us been told that youth is the time for forming good habits, and nothing could be truer.

In the chapter on the Brain and Nervous system we saw how it is that habits are formed. Every action, while it is doing, makes what we may call a track in the brain and nerve threads concerned, so that each performance of it is easier than the last, till, in the case of actions we have occasion to perform very often, we need put forth no conscious effort at all.

Every day each of us is strengthening or weakening old habits—perhaps beginning new ones. The weakening of an old habit is a very difficult matter, whether for good or for evil, so that those who have all along trained themselves to do what is right grow stronger and stronger in a good life and those who have allowed and still allow themselves in what is wrong are every day making a return to the right more difficult and painful to accomplish.

Now, at first sight, it may seem as if there were a great number of good habits to be formed, and a great number of bad habits to be avoided. On looking deeper into the matter, however, we shall find that one habit is often caused by another; and, on going back from effect to cause, we shall discover at last just one or two good habits which are the foundation of good character, and one or two bad habits which undermine character and may practically destroy it.

In this chapter we will consider that specially good habit which has most to do with health and its contrary, which causes many injuries to health.

Industry

The good habit I mean is that of Industry.

We may fairly say that protoplasm is the highest, most wonderful, and most beautiful substance known to us; more than that, it has in it possibilities of which no imagination can see the end. If we consider, on the one hand, the little, one-celled animals and plants which the microscope shows us in a drop of dew or of sea-water, and, on the other, such a man as Shakespeare or Isaac Newton, we see what marvellous powers living substance has already developed.

Now what I want you to think over, to try and realize is this: That the long, long ascent, through millions and millions of years, from the lowly beginnings of life to the mind of the greatest of men, was achieved by one principal means—by movement, by constant activity. Those creatures which were inert perished, degenerated, or remained as they were; those which were active improved their sense-organs, their nervous system, the respiratory system which supplied them with energy, and the muscles and limbs which enabled them to move yet more rapidly. Some improved in one way, some in another, but it was always the most active which improved the most, and became more and more the masters of the world.

When man appeared the same great law of activity was seen in still greater force. The races of men who were active multiplied and grew stronger and stronger. They conquered wild beasts; they conquered feebler tribes of men; they made weapons, tools, houses; they developed speech and invented writing. They tamed animals, they learnt the use of fire and of metals; they learnt how to take care of herds, how to cook, to sow and plant, and how to cross the sea.

All these things took untold years to accomplish; and the tribes which were active learnt and practised them, while the inactive tribes dwindled away.

We need not pursue this progress of man any further here—you may trace it for yourself in your history, where a very little thought will show you that the men and races who have been energetic and eager for movement have always triumphed over the indolent.

To acquire the habit of industry, then, really means to obey one of the great laws by which all advance of any kind has been made—the law of movement, of activity. There is no greater disgrace than that of leading an idle life. It matters not, whether they be rich or poor, of high or of low estate, the men and women who are idle are literally the undoing of humanity for, so far as in them lies, they hinder what the workers all around them are striving to accomplish.

Different Kinds of Work

Many people think that those whom we call working-people, labourers and artisans, labour the most and work the longest hours. But this is by no means the case. The hardest of all work is the work of the brain; and there are thousands of men and women engaged in such work who have far less leisure than those whose work is manual or muscular.

Just as in our own bodies the different cells composing different organs do different work, and each organ is necessary to the others and to the body as a whole—so we ourselves cannot do without one another. We need all the various kinds of honest work which men and women do, and no one ought to despise his neighbour's. Those who work with the head should respect those who labour with their hands. Men should respect the work of women, and women that of men. And all alike should know something of the deeds of those greatest toilers of the world whom, very few of us can ever hope to approach, but whose work we should love and rejoice in nevertheless. Such among many other Englishmen are Priestley, Faraday, Lyell, Herschel. Above all, the boys and girls of England

FIGURE 33 — T. H. HUXLEY

should remember Thomas Henry Huxley, who did so much both for science and for education.

Recreation

Perhaps someone will say in answer to this, that all work and no play makes Jack a dull boy; that we cannot be always working, we must have some recreation and some rest.

That is quite true. We saw in the chapter about the brain that recreation and rest are both necessary. But those who have acquired the habit of industry take their recreation in a manner very different from the slothful.

If we are always busy and interested in something we value our time too much to squander it on any poor, stupid sort of employment, still less shall we waste it in "loafing" and doing nothing.

Our recreations will be most often of the nature of a hobby. We may set ourselves to acquire skill in some sort of game or in some handicraft; we may take up some branch of natural science and learn all we can about it; we may give our leisure time to pictures, or music, to the study of ancient buildings, or to gardening.

It does not matter much what the hobby is, provided that it is sensible and injures nobody, and is also sufficiently distinct from our main work in life to afford us refreshment.

Men and women whose work keeps them sitting indoors should have hobbies which take them out into the open air and give them exercise. Those whose chief work gives them plenty of out-door exercise, and perhaps requires little effort of the brain to do thoroughly, may well choose hobbies which will involve reading and close thinking.

Between working hard at our calling, doing our duty cheerfully in our own household and in our own village or town, and pursuing some favourite hobby, we shall find the days almost too short for all there is to be done in them. Habit will make this activity a most delightful necessity to us.

There is no happiness in the world greater, more lasting, and more satisfying than that of knowing one has accomplished good work—has put out all one's strength and done one's very best—and this happiness is the daily experience of the industrious, no matter what their work may be.

If you want an instance of what industry and the pursuit of a hobby can accomplish you should read the life of Hugh Miller, the great geologist, who began by being a stone-mason. He has told it himself most beautifully in his book "My Schools and Schoolmasters."

FIGURE 34 — HUGH MILLER

What Industry has to do with Health

But what has this habit of industry to do with health? It has very much to do with it.

In the first place that very happiness of which we

have just spoken is one of the finest things in the world for health.

In the second place the habit of industry nearly always causes us to form a number of other habits which are wholesome such as those of early rising, temperance in eating and drinking, cleanliness, thoroughness in all we do, interest in things outside ourselves, thrift and a love of order.

And in the third place, the habit of industry saves us from many temptations. "Idleness is the root of all evil." As we shall see in a moment, most of the troubles and sufferings of men can be traced back to a root in idle habits.

Evils of Idleness

Idleness, or inactivity, makes us weak.

If we do not use our powers of thought they will dwindle away. If we do not exercise our power of will we shall find we can no longer make ourselves do what is right; nor resist evil influences. If we work or play half-heartedly, instead of with all our might, we shall lose the power of doing things thoroughly and the power of keen enjoyment.

The idle mind may at last become so weak and so dreary that it takes pleasure in nothing.

In the same way, if the body, as a whole, is allowed to be inactive, it becomes feeble. Muscles which are insufficiently exercised grow stiff and powerless.

Constant sitting or lounging, and the lack of brisk movement, will deprive the organs of their vigour. Without a due amount of general bodily activity the lungs cannot draw deep breaths, the food-pipe digests with difficulty, the blood moves sluggishly along its course, and waste matters are got rid of slowly and incompletely.

The body, being thus enfeebled, has little power of resistance, and disease may easily get the upper hand; while in a similar way the mind, which sloth has made weak, becomes a ready prey to all kinds of folly and of wickedness.

Idle people shirk their work. Hence they run the risk of being blamed, perhaps punished; and to avoid this they fall into a habit of untruthfulness and petty deceits.

Being interested in nothing particular, they are on the look-out for excitement and pastimes; and hence we find many idlers fall into the habit of gambling. Gambling is the cause of many evils which we cannot dwell on in this book; but we may remember that it is destructive of all the finest and best powers of the mind. The brain and nervous system, which are constantly employed in this unworthy occupation, become in time incapable of true work or true happiness; and in this way many a man and woman who might have led a noble and useful life has been ruined and degraded.

Another bad habit formed among the idle is that of incessant talking. Gossip and chatter never did anything to help good work. We never find that any great worker ever left off what he was doing to stand and indulge himself in idle chat; and none who let this habit grow upon them will make successful men or women.

Idle people are often the source of great discomfort to those who are connected with them. They are bad workmen, wasting their own time and other people's without accomplishing anything satisfactory. They are sometimes stingy, because they cannot be at the pains to find out how best to spend their money; and sometimes spendthrift, because they cannot take the trouble to deny themselves anything they fancy. The habit of selfishness, of seeking one's own ease, and brooding over one's own troubles or grievances, nearly always goes with idleness; and this habit not only hinders the idler from making any true progress, but also makes life more difficult for other people.

By a little reflection you will easily discover several more bad habits which spring from the habit of idleness. We must now go on to speak of two in particular which have perhaps a more direct effect upon health than any others.

Smoking

The first of these habits is that of smoking tobacco, especially in the form of cigarettes.

The leaves from which tobacco is prepared contain a substance called **Nicotine**, in itself a deadly poison. When smoking it is, of course, only a very small quantity of nicotine which is taken into the blood; yet even this small quantity is harmful, especially to the young.

In the first place, it injures the brain and nerves. The pleasant, dreamy sensation which accompanies smoking is simply caused by the nervous system being benumbed. Now, while the nerve-cells are still young this numbness is not merely a temporary state soon overcome, it causes real damage to the tissues, and if often repeated will prevent the proper development of the brain and nervous system from ever taking place.

Next, tobacco renders the muscles incapable of rapid or accurate action, for, as we have seen, they depend on impulse and control from the nerves, and thus when the nerves are weakened they also lose their vigour. Lack of nervous control makes the heart beat too fast, and it is further injured by the poverty of the blood which tobacco causes.

Smoking is also bad for the digestion. Most people are made aware of this on their first attempt at it. They feel very sick, and, no doubt, if it were not for bad example and fashion, this protest of Nature would prevent them from trying again. After the feeling of sickness has worn off, however, tobacco still interferes with digestion, injuring the nerves of the stomach and causing the teeth to decay.

Any thoughtful boy, recollecting what we have learned about the food-pipe, about the nerves, and about the circulation, will be able to reckon up for himself the consequences of smoking to a person who has not yet done growing.

Since smoking hinders nutrition, and since without

nutrition there can be no proper growth, it follows that boy smokers are very likely to be stunted.

Such, in fact, we find them for the most part: pale, small, weakly, dull in their brains. Those of them who are comparatively bright and strong are yet not what they might have been if they had never contracted this most mistaken habit.

No one under twenty-one ought to smoke at all. It is the first twenty years of a man's life which determine whether he is to be strong, well-grown, healthy and muscular, whether his senses are to be keen, and his brain active; or whether he is to be poor in health, with blunted senses and little mental power. Is it worth while to sacrifice one's chances of vigour, happiness, and success in life to the temporary pleasure—if it is even good enough to be called a pleasure—of lounging about with a cigarette in one's mouth? Surely no sensible boy, no young man who means to make his mark in the world, can possibly think it so.

The more boys there are in a country who thus enfeeble themselves, the weaker must the country itself become; and those who have the welfare of England most at heart are beginning to grow anxious as they see how much very young boys now indulge themselves in the habit of smoking.

After twenty-one years of age the body no longer has to undergo so great a strain of growth, and the tissues have more resisting power. Hence, if smoking be begun then it is not necessarily injurious, provided it be strictly moderate. Intemperate smoking, however, is harmful at any time of life, partly from its effect on the constitution, and partly because it commonly makes idle habits worse, and so renders the man more and more useless.

Alcohol

The second bad habit is one far more dreadful and dangerous—one which has been the ruin of many happy homes and of many promising lives.

You will guess that I mean the habit of taking alcohol.

We will not dwell here on the terrible misery and degradation of the drunkard, nor on the crimes committed through drunkenness by men who in their sober state would never have injured anyone, nor yet on the bitter sufferings which this evil habit brings upon so many innocent and deserving people. All this is known only too well.

What we want to think of now is, how it is that alcohol produces these terrible effects upon those who indulge themselves in it.

This book has been written to very little purpose if you have not realized that no part of the body is of such importance to us as the brain. Anything which harms the brain is peculiarly terrible and grievous.

Even a small injury or a little weakening of its vigour is something to be sorry for and to avoid; what shall we say, then, of the actual destruction of that wonderful organ upon which so much depends?

The first thing to fix firmly in our minds concerning alcohol is that it is peculiarly dangerous to the brain and the whole nervous system.

Now, many people suppose that to take a small quantity of alcohol is beneficial rather than otherwise. They may tell us it makes their brain work better; that they have a fine flow of ideas, and feel great energy of thought. But this sensation is really produced by the effect of alcohol upon the nerves which regulate the arteries. They allow the arteries to relax so that the blood pours into them more freely and this rush of blood into the brain causes excitement, while at the same time there is a feeling of warmth over the whole body. But this very excitement, this rush of ideas, is in reality due to loss of control, and it has been proved over and over again that it lasts for only about fifteen minutes. Towards the end of that time the work of the brain becomes more and more full of errors; then it grows slower, and at last the labour is more difficult to the brain than it was before the alcohol was taken. Hence we find that the habitual drinker becomes slovenly in his work and in his person, and loses self-control. This will often mean losing his employment and his regular wages, and drifting down into a miserable hand-to-mouth kind of life.

It is therefore a mistake to suppose that a small quantity of alcohol is of any assistance in intellectual occupations, while the effect of constantly applying the stimulus is disastrous.

If a large quantity of alcohol is drunk the excitement

of the brain becomes greater and greater, and the bulb and spinal cord begin to be affected. Hence the man walks very uncertainly, and cannot control his movements; his thoughts are muddled, and he is angry, or boisterously merry, without reason or the power to check himself.

After further drinking, the whole brain is affected. Now the man can hardly move or see; thought and will disappear. If yet more alcohol is taken, the whole nervous system is poisoned, and the man becomes entirely unconscious and unable to stir. Should the heart and lungs escape, he may recover; but if the nerves by which these are worked are paralysed, then the result must be death.

There are many men who do not often, perhaps do not ever, sink to this last stage of drunkenness, but yet are very frequently intoxicated in a lesser degree. In these we may see another grievous consequence of drink. The alcohol taken is never quite got rid of, and so remains as a poison in the blood. It sets up most destructive changes in the tissues of the nerves and brain, and these frequently end in producing insanity.

This is only a very brief and imperfect account of the harm done by alcohol to the brain and nervous system. If there were nothing more to be told, surely this in itself should be enough to make every man or woman pause before they indulge themselves in a thoughtless inclination for any kind of intoxicating liquor.

Effect of Alcohol on the Heart and Circulatory System

But the damage to the brain and nervous system is by no means the only danger of alcohol.

It is also exceedingly injurious to the heart and the circulatory system. After long-continued drinking the muscular tissue which forms the wall of the heart becomes fatty, and loses its power. Anything which weakens the heart causes a sensation of great depression and misery; and this sometimes makes a man drink more and more. The heart may be thus rendered so feeble that it has no longer force enough to drive the blood onward; and, as you know, when the heart stops working life must come to an end.

Similar changes take place in the walls of the blood-vessels, so that the circulation is thrown out of order. If this destructive process goes on, the arteries may become too weak to resist the pressure of the blood, and may burst. The bursting of an artery in the brain may mean death.

On the Food-pipe

In the food-pipe alcohol is no less mischievous. The nerves and glands of the stomach are so injuriously affected by it that the flow of gastric juice is diminished, and the juice itself has little power. Further, the muscular wall of the stomach becomes stiffer and thicker; and while the powers of digestion are thus disabled, the food itself is made more difficult to digest, for alcohol has a hardening effect on protein substances.

Even worse is the damage which alcohol does to the liver. It irritates the delicate gland-cells, and sets up fatty degeneration in them; and later on, if drinking is persisted in, produces a hardening and shrinking of the whole substance of the liver, which makes it entirely useless and causes terrible forms of disease.

Other Ill Effects of Alcohol

You may think that this is surely all there is to say of the harm done by alcohol. No, there is yet far more. I might tell you how it weakens the muscles, and so spoils their tissues as to make delicate adjustment of them impossible, so that no drunkard can do fine, highly-skilled work. I have described to you how it weakens the tissue of the lungs; how it injures the sense of touch in the skin, causes inflammation of the kidneys, and robs the body of that heat which, as you know, is the source of our energy.

But surely it is unnecessary to go into any further sad details; surely it is impossible that any girls or boys who have learnt, though but in outline, what a wonderful and beautiful structure is the human body, should need more than this to convince them how lamentable and dangerous an evil is the use of alcohol.

It has, of course, been known for generations that an excessive use of wine and beer and spirits does great harm, brings on disease, ruins the character, in many cases causes death.

But many scientific men now find that even a small quantity of alcohol is harmful; that the use of it steadily weakens the body in every way, and leaves it more defenceless against disease.

So that for those whose minds are open to new knowledge, alcohol must henceforth count much as those drugs which we buy at the chemist's. These we may have to take now and again when ordered to do so by a doctor, but, if we are sensible, we shall never take them without such advice.

Alcoholic Drinks a Relic of Barbarism

It is a good thing to bear in mind that the use of alcoholic drinks is in reality a relic of old and barbarous times.

All savage peoples have discovered the way to make intoxicating liquors of some kind, whether from fruits, or corn, or honey, and all seek the excitement produced by these.

The continued use of them has been said to mark an imperfect civilization. If this is so, it would seem that we English people have no right to pride ourselves greatly on our state of civilization. We ought, on the contrary, to consider very humbly how we may do away with an evil which is keeping large numbers of us in a more or less barbarous state. Indeed, until we have freed ourselves from the hold that alcohol has over us as a nation, there does not seem much point in our boasted liberty—in our declaring that "Britons never, never shall be slaves." It is less degrading to be subject to men of another nation than it is to be subject to an evil habit, which sinks many a man and woman far lower than the animals. And this latter subjection is also by far the harder to throw off.

Why People Take to Drink

Why is it that people, as we say, take to drink? Some do it out of fatigue; some to drown worry or grief; others out of excitement; others because they feel dull and heavy and want rousing; others, again, out of sheer idleness, because they can think of nothing better to do. Many make the sad mistake of supposing that what is a poison is a form of food; and many more are brought to take it by bad example, fashion, fear of ridicule, and an absurd desire to appear manly.

Yet another cause, which is especially common among women and girls, is the habit of taking quack medicines. These are many of them most pernicious; they may allay pain and seem to do good for a time, but they often injure the constitution more than the original trouble they are taken to cure. The remedy being thus worse than the disease, the sufferer, when she begins to feel the weakening effect of the drug, often commits the grievous error of taking some alcoholic stimulant to make her feel stronger and more comfortable. Now that you know something about the nature of the body, you can understand how dangerous it is to be taking drugs in a haphazard way.

What, then, can we do to guard against the operation of these different causes?

Industry a Remedy for the Drinking Habit

So far as the habit of drinking is begun and kept up out of sheer dulness and emptiness of mind—and this cause is, indeed, one of the most frequent of all—we shall find that it can be counteracted by the habit of industry, which we considered at the beginning of this chapter.

A man or woman whose mind is full of lively thoughts and interests, who is constantly busy in some profitable occupation, will at least never take to drink from not knowing what else to do. In all probability drink will hardly be a temptation to such a one.

More than this, industry, as we have seen, strengthens the will and the whole character, so that if, from some other cause, the temptation to drink arises, there will be found a hundredfold more strength to resist it in the industrious than in the idle.

Industry, again—bodily activity and a keen interest in different pursuits—will draw off much of that temptation to drink which comes from excitement. In fact, as the ordinary safeguard of the ordinary day and its temptations, the habit of industry, if we will only take care to make it strong enough, will commonly see us through.

Other Causes of the Drinking Habit

Let us take next those who fly to drink to give them relief from fatigue.

Here, again, we must get back to causes. Very often indeed, the sense of utter weariness which brings on the great temptation is not due to hard work—or not to hard work alone. Very often it is due to an overcrowded home, to breathing poisonous air, to the general discomfort and disorder in which some people live. Another cause, not by any means sufficiently reckoned with, is indigestion from ill-cooked or hastily eaten food, as well as from food which, being highly seasoned or salted, irritates the taste-buds and causes great thirst.

Then we must not forget that evil tempers, nagging, worry, and unkindness cause great depression and great fatigue, both in those who inflict and those who have to endure this kind of misery.

Any doctor will tell you that hard work rarely or never hurts an ordinarily healthy person; it is worry or something wrong with their surroundings which does the real harm.

Now what are the remedies for this state of things?

The public remedy lies in securing better houses, more room, more air, and sunshine for those who live in the crowded parts of our towns and in the more ill-provided places in the country.

In a later chapter we shall see what a healthy home

should be like, and everyone ought to try to obtain such a home both for himself and for his neighbours.

But there are also remedies which lie more immediately within our power. Part of them are in the hands of the women and girls of the family; part in the hands of the men and boys. It would take too much space to go into all the details which might be mentioned, but we will take one or two of each kind.

First of all, women ought to regard the management of a household and the preparation of the food in the same way as a good workman regards his craft, or a good professional man his profession. They ought to require of themselves real skill and accuracy of method in everything they do. More than that, they ought to be always ready to learn how to do things better and better. Science, which has opened up so many new methods in every kind of work, has a great deal to say about cooking and the management of a house. When all housewives are, so far as their work goes, skilled and scientific, all homes will be far more healthy and comfortable than they are now.

Secondly, those women and girls who are most earnest and most conscientious about their home duties should remember that there is after all a big world outside the four walls of their house. They should come out into it as often as they can; they should learn something of public matters, something of what other women in other countries or divisions of society are doing; they should busy their minds with the discoveries, the events, and the interests which reach beyond the welfare of their own individual family. The danger of a woman's life within doors is that she may grow low-spirited or narrow-minded, not able to distinguish between the things that are little and the things that are big, and so may come to worry herself and those around her about matters of no importance.

If the women manage the house and prepare the food well and skillfully, men should do their share by attending to the fabric of the house. They should see that all is in good order, that the drains are sound and well laid, that there is a sufficient water supply, and sufficient light. They should also give a helping hand in household affairs.

One of the saddest causes of drink is hunger; and any man who, by idling away his time, or by squandering money when he has earned it, leaves his wife and children to hunger, is the one who is responsible if any one of them falls into the habit of drinking.

Besides this, men should remember that women's work is more monotonous for the most part than men's, and therefore men should take care that women have their share of pleasure and variety.

If we all attend to these things—if we see to it that our households have good food, peace, and plenty of fresh air, we shall be doing more than most people realize to diminish the temptation to drink.

CHAPTER XI

FOOD AND COOKING

*"Diet well ordered bears the greatest part
in the prolongation of life."*

— Francis Bacon

Those of you who have had anything to do with animals know how eager they are about their food. So are we, perhaps you will say; and that is quite true.

Men and animals alike depend on food for energy, nourishment, and life itself, so that it is no wonder they both are much occupied with all that relates to it.

In a wild state the greater part of an animal's life is divided between searching for food, eating it when found, and digesting it. For instance, how many birds and mammals we see expending immense energy in movement—flying, hopping, running, leaping, climbing, and so on! On looking closer we find that they are all simply hunting for flies, worms, mice, juicy leaves, buds, seeds,—in fact, for whatever the particular food of each may be.

As they thus spend a great amount of energy in hunting, so they also spend a good deal in digesting

201

their food. Because an animal lies still, perhaps fast asleep, it does not follow that its body is doing nothing. On the contrary, it is often the work of digestion going on in the food-pipe which prevents the animal from doing anything else, by absorbing for the time the whole of its powers.

Here is a point in which men differ from animals. Men think about many things besides their food, and engage in innumerable occupations which are not, in themselves, connected with eating or drinking.

How has this become possible?

One of the chief causes of the difference is the fact that a man need not spend nearly so great a proportion of his energy on the digestion of his food as an animal is compelled to do. Hence the man has energy to spare for other things.

And why is this? Principally because men have learnt to prepare their food, so as to render it easy to digest. Animals eat their food as they find it; men have learnt to cook.

Some people dislike cooking, and seem to think themselves too fine for such work. This is a very foolish notion.

We must remember that it is by division of labour among the cells that the bodies of living creatures have grown more and more active, and perfect in their different parts.

It is also by division of labour among men that nations are enabled to rise to greater and greater things.

In this division of labour, all the work connected with providing and preparing food is as necessary to a nation as the work of the food-pipe is to the individual body. If such work is badly done among a people, everybody suffers, and they lose some of the advantages of the division of labour.

Now, from this I hope you will see what a great office is that of the housekeeper and the cook—of the person, be it man or woman, who chooses the food of the household, and prepares it for the meal.

Everyone to whom this work falls may well be proud. It is given to her, or to him, to furnish the means by which the body is built up and kept in energy. But more than this, it is the carefully cooked, easily digested food which gives man the spare energy for work and thought, and so enables him to raise himself above the level of the ordinary animal.

Kinds of Food

The kinds of food, as we saw in the chapter on the food-pipe, are five: proteins, starches and sugars, fats, mineral matters, and water.

The **proteins** are substances which, you will remember, contain all the chief elements of protoplasm, and notably **nitrogen**, which is the element most required for building up the tissues of the body.

When separated off from the rest of the food-stuffs in which they occur, proteins, as we have already seen, appear in the form of curd. The curd of milk is an instance of this; and other very similar proteins are the white and the yolk of egg. Fish and the lean of meat contain a very large proportion of protein, and so does cheese.

You can separate out the protein in flour by mixing some flour with water, so as to make a dough, and then washing this dough in water again and again. A whitish substance—the starch—will come away in the washing, and you will find left in your hands a sticky, toughish, grey lump. This is the curd-like protein.

If you were to burn these different substances— the curd of milk, white of egg, yolk of egg, meat, fish, and the stringy remainder of your dough—you would find they had all the same strong, unpleasant smell in burning, like that of burnt feathers. This is due to the presence in them of nitrogen.

We must remember that we cannot live without nitrogen: hence we cannot live without protein food. Any form of food which contains protein is therefore particularly valuable. The food-stuffs which contain it in the largest proportion are, as I told you before, lean of meat, fish, eggs, cheese, and milk. It is also found, though in smaller proportion, in oatmeal and flour, and in such vegetables as lentils, beans, and peas.

Starches and **sugars** are found in the different grains, and in some of the roots that we use. Beetroot, carrots, and turnips contain sugar; wheat, rice, arrowroot, and potato contain starch. These substances, being largely composed of carbon, give us heat, and the energy which depends on heat.

The **fats** are like the starches in so far that they also furnish us with heat and energy. Unlike the starches, they also contribute something to the building up of the body. They are especially needed by the nervous system. Butter and bacon are the two most digestible forms of fat; but dripping is exceedingly useful, and so is margarine—as sold in Germany and Belgium.

It was Lavoisier, the great French chemist, who first discovered that fats and starches, being largely composed of carbon, combine with the oxygen in the body, and thus keep up a constant burning. He, too, found out that the heat of this burning, of which more has been said in the chapter on respiration, is the source of our energy.

FIGURE 35 — LAVOISIER, THE GREAT FRENCH CHEMIST

We further need certain **mineral substances** to keep us healthy. These are principally obtained by eating green vegetables and fruit. You will find in the chapter on the food-pipe yet another reason why we should eat plenty of these latter kinds of food. Fruit and vegetables should always be as fresh as possible, and are more wholesome cooked than raw, because of the presence of bacteria and other parasites.

Finally, we must not forget that we cannot live without water. All the substances we use as food contain a great deal of water, but it is a good thing to drink plenty of it besides. Two things should be attended to with regard to this: first, **water for drinking should be boiled for at least ten minutes**; secondly, we should drink water at the end of a meal or between meals—not during, still less before beginning, a meal.

A careful, sensible housekeeper will be at great pains to observe the right proportion in the different kinds of foods she provides for her household. She will not give them building-up food alone, nor heat-giving food alone.

In the proportion suitable to an average person the starch and sugar should be four times as much as the proteins, and ten times as much as the fats.

But while keeping this proportion in mind we should always consider for whom we are buying food, since persons of different ages and occupations require to have it slightly altered to suit their different needs.

Food for Children

Children require plenty of fat in their food. The surface of a child's body is much greater in proportion to its bulk than is that of a grown-up person, hence there is a greater escape of heat which has to be made good. A tall, thin child for the same reason wants more heating food than a short, stout one. Besides some difference in proportion, children need a much greater quantity of all kinds of food than grown-up people do, in comparison with their size and the lack of food is more injurious to them. You need hardly be told the reason of this; your own sense will tell you that it is because the food of children has not only to repair the waste caused by their activity, but also to provide material for their growth.

There are, however, many children who are provided with sufficient food, very good of its kind, yet do not thrive as one might expect. This is sometimes due to the not uncommon mistake of giving them too great a proportion of starch and too small a proportion of fat and protein. They get too many potatoes, perhaps, and too little meat; too much bread, and too little butter. Another mistake is that of giving them their starchy food in too soft and pappy a form. Such food is not bitten up, but is quickly swallowed; hence it is not properly mingled with saliva, and the starch is unaltered and very indigestible. Little children should be given stale bread, crusts, chippy toast, rusks and tolerably hard biscuits, rather than cakes and new bread. Biting these will make the saliva flow freely and mingle with the

207

starch. Moreover, this exercise will greatly strengthen the teeth; and I may here mention that the teeth suffer very much when they do not get enough work to do.

Food for Muscular Work

The food needed by a grown man or woman whose employment is chiefly muscular must be planned differently from that of the child. Now, English working people often make the mistake of thinking that a person who has to use his muscles a great deal should eat plenty of meat. On the contrary, meat is not specially necessary for him—he should rather take plenty of starchy and sugary food, and get much of the protein he wants from peas, lentils, or beans. Fish and cheese are also good for him; but he need use meat only in small quantities. If he wants to see a proof of this he should look abroad, where he will find the German and French workman using haricot beans, the American and Italian using maize and macaroni, and the Japanese, the strongest man of all, using rice, to which he adds a little fish or a hard-boiled egg as protein. This diet gives strength and energy, and is more wholesome than meat, besides being very much cheaper.

Of all foods for the man or boy who uses his muscles none is better than sugar, for it gives the muscles both energy and endurance. The mountaineers in Switzerland take plenty of sweet chocolate with them on their expeditions for this reason. The advantages of the use of sugar have also been shown by experiments in the German army.

Anyone whose digestion is weak should, however, be careful in the use of sugar, for though so serviceable in itself, it is apt to cause indigestion.

Food for Brain Work

When our work is not so much muscular as brainwork, and chiefly sedentary, it is very important that our food should be easy to digest; first, because we want to leave as much energy as possible free for thought; secondly, because movement of the abdominal muscles helps digestion, and the brain-worker must do without much of this help. Muscular exertion is particularly useful in the digestion of such foods as beans and lentils, and therefore the brain-worker must not have his protein in this form, but rather in small quantities of meat or fish, which are easier to digest. The brain, like the rest of the body, cannot do without food, but it is an error to suppose that there is any particular food which specially nourishes the brain. We should further remember that no part of the body suffers more than the brain does if we make the mistake of over-eating. If we give the body more nitrogen than it can use, the excess acts as a kind of poison, hindering all the organs in their work, and hindering none so much as the brain.

Food for the Old

The diet of old people should be sparing; over-feeding is dangerous for them, because in old age the body can neither digest so well nor get rid of waste matter so well as it did in youth and middle life. Fats and proteins should be somewhat reduced in proportion to the rest of their food, and whatever they eat should be light and easily digested. It is good for them to have small quantities of food at short intervals rather than bigger meals at fairly long intervals, such as suit younger persons.

Easily Digested Foods

Perhaps you will now ask what is meant by easily digested food. It is food which the stomach has little trouble in churning into chyme, and of which the proteins may readily be dissolved out by the gastric juice. Such food is soon ready to pass out into the intestine. Of course, it does not always follow that a food which is very easy to digest contains the greatest amount of nourishment; it is in many cases worth while to give the stomach somewhat more trouble in order to obtain more energy and more heat. But in aged people, and in those who are delicate, or perhaps temporarily ailing, the stomach is usually incapable of doing hard work, and must be spared as much as possible.

The most easily digested foods are: Mutton, steamed

fish, eggs lightly boiled, fat bacon (especially cold), butter, junket, milk (diluted with half boiled water or soda-water or lime-water), biscuits, thin toast, crust of bread, stale bread, Hovis and malt bread, mashed potatoes, macaroni (well cooked), and stewed fruit.

On the other hand everyone whose digestion is not strong should avoid pork, veal, sausages, duck, goose, pastry, rich cakes, unripe fruit, raw onions, undiluted milk, any very fatty foods, and fresh bread.

Milk for Babes

Little babies under six months old ought to have nothing but milk. Before that age the food-pipe is not yet provided with teeth to grind up the food, nor with all the juices which act on starch; therefore to feed a baby on sopped bread or rice or potato, or anything starchy, is in reality starving it, as well as causing it very great suffering. If cow's milk is used it should be boiled and then diluted with boiled water, or well-boiled barley-water, or, better still, lime-water. If this disagrees with the baby, or it does not thrive, a doctor should be asked what had best be done.

Patent foods should be used with caution, and only along with other kinds of food. For one thing, children fed on these alone do not get a sufficient amount of fat, and fat is, as we have seen, a very important part of their diet. Although sometimes advertised as inexpensive, patent foods prove very costly.

Variety in Food

A good housekeeper will take a pleasure in studying what are the tastes of the people whose food she has to plan—at least, so far as their tastes are wholesome. Variety should also be considered; it is, in fact, very necessary. Several men of science have tried upon themselves the experiment of living on only one or two kinds of food, and the results showed how injurious this may be.

So do not try to live on nothing but bread and butter and tea. If you do so your poor body will become weaker and weaker, and will easily fall a prey to those invisible enemies of which I told you in the last chapter.

How to Live Cheaply

Perhaps, however, someone will say, "It is all very well to tell us we must have good food, and must have variety, but what can one do if one has only a very little money?"

Now, in the first place, we ought to realize that nothing we have to spend money upon is nearly so important as food. It comes before any clothing, except the most absolutely necessary, and far, far before furniture or any of those ornaments or nick-nacks of different kinds with which we sometimes like to decorate ourselves or our houses. As for tobacco and alcohol in any form, to get these with money that is needed to buy food is a most grievous kind of madness.

So if you find yourself short of money, stint yourself and your household in anything rather than in good food. Good food will give all of you a warmth and energy which will make other discomforts lighter and enable you to work hard and bring back better days; it will keep up your power of resisting the bacteria which attack those who are weak, and it will preserve you from the bad effects of worry.

The most false of all kinds of false economy is that which attempts to save by stinting in food.

At the same time we must remember that cheap food, if it be fresh and good of its kind, is as serviceable as dear food, sometimes more so. Dr. Edward Smith tells us that among animal foods the despised herring or bloater offers the largest amount of nourishment for a given sum. Two salt herrings furnish as much animal protein as is required by a working man in the course of a day. Margarine may not be as pleasant to the taste as butter, but it will give you almost the same amount of warmth and energy. It is a pity that so many people have a prejudice against margarine, as it is now made from pure fats, and is, in the true sense of the word, an economical food.

If English meat is somewhat too expensive for our purse, we can buy "chilled" New Zealand meat, which has precisely the same qualities and nourishment.

Then, again, the cheaper cuts of meat are no worse than the dearer from the point of view of true food. Brisket of beef, for instance, if bought fresh, not salted, and carefully stewed with vegetables, not only makes a pleasant and inexpensive dish, but will build up the body as effectively as the sirloin. If you cannot buy meat very often, you can still obtain protein from lentils and beans; while cheese is one of the most excellent foods, and a cheap cheese may be quite as good as a dear one. Other building-up materials which cost very little are skim-milk and buttermilk. The fat has been removed from them, but the protein remains. Both are very digestible, and it has been calculated that half a pint of buttermilk contains as much nourishment as 2 oz. of bread. Another very nourishing form of food is the banana, with its store of starch, and this can often be bought for very little.

So do not think that because an article of food is cheap it is therefore to be despised as poor stuff. We might learn much from our neighbour on the Continent with regard to this. Among all of them the bulk of the population has much less money to spend than with us, and yet they have good food, in many cases better prepared than ours. I should advise any one of my readers who has anything to do with housekeeping to try and find out how French and German people manage their food. There is a great deal that is interesting and helpful to be learnt from them.

Anyone who thoroughly understands the qualities of each kind of food, and buys her provisions accordingly, may feed a household as well on a very little money as the richest people can be fed at great expense; for, after all, what we pay for in the more costly kinds of food is principally flavour, and not any increase in those strengthening and energy-giving properties of food which are essential to life.

I may just mention one or two articles of food which are extravagant, because the amount of nourishment they supply is very small in proportion to their cost. Such are the various extracts of meat and beef-tea. The use of these is to stimulate the appetite, especially in sickness. They are not, properly speaking, foods at all, for they do not build up the body. If mixed with milk they are, of course, really nourishing, but far from economical.

Other such articles are cornflour and custard powders. These are simply starch, which, in the latter case, is mixed with colouring matter, not with eggs. The proteins and fatty substances of the flour have been washed away, so that there is very little nourishment obtained in return for the money spent on them.

Cooking: Meat and Fish

Next we come to the question of how to cook our food; for the best food in the world will be indigestible and harmful if badly cooked. If we always have in mind the principles and the reasons which underlie cooking we shall work much more successfully.

Let us begin with meat and fish. We cook these substances in order to make them more tasty rather than more digestible.

By cooking meat carefully we bring out its flavour, and we also make the connective tissue which wraps the muscle soft and jelly-like. Heat hardens the protein of the meat, just as it sets the liquid white of egg. When hardened beyond a very slight degree the protein becomes flavourless and very indigestible. So we must give a little thought to the question of how to apply the heat successfully.

The most economical way of cooking meat is **stewing**, for in this method none of the juices of the meat are lost. The best way of stewing is to get a pudding-basin, and put into it the meat you want to cook, together with a little rice and some vegetable— such as potato, carrot, turnip, onion, or tomato, cut into pieces. A little water, or better still, a little stock, should be added—the quantity must depend on the juiciness of the meat and the nature of the vegetables. Having added a little salt and pepper, cover the basin with a plate, and stand it in a saucepan of boiling water to steam for some hours. You will find the result delicious as well as nourishing.

In **baking** meat the double object is, first, to harden the outer surface, so that it may form a kind of seal and keep in the juices of the meat; and then to cook the inside of the joint gently, so that no flavour or nourishment may be lost. We should therefore put our meat into a good hot oven to start with, and after a short time reduce the heat.

Boiling should be done on the same principle. Plunge the joint at once into boiling water, and keep it boiling for a minute, so as to harden the outside and prevent the escape of the juices into the water. Then draw the saucepan to the side of the fire, and let the rest of the cooking go on slowly.

Fish should be steamed, or fried in hot fat. The former method is the more digestible. Boiled in water fresh fish loses its flavour and valuable juices.

Starchy Foods

On starchy foods we find that cooking has a far more important effect. Nothing is more indigestible than uncooked starch of whatever sort, and it is a great unkindness to serve such food for anyone to eat.

When examined through the microscope, starch is seen to be composed of tiny grains, enclosed in a case or framework. Now this framework cannot be digested, and it prevents the digestive juices from getting at the nourishing food within the starch-grains. You will remember that cold water cannot dissolve starch; but if we apply heat to the water in which the starch is mixed we can make the starch soluble. Heat causes the grains to swell and burst the framework. This is why, on boiling cornflour or arrowroot, you find it expand, and form a thick soft pulp; it shows you also how your potatoes and your rice get soft when you cook them—the starch grains in each have burst, and let the starch loose. The effect of dry heat upon the starch is to make it soluble by bringing about a change in its substance. We need not dwell further on this here, except to mention that it is this which makes biscuits and thin toast particularly easy to digest.

Bread

Your teacher of cookery will be able to give you many interesting recipes for all kinds of good cakes and puddings and I hope you will learn to make at least the easier ones. A suet pudding, if it is light and thoroughly boiled, is excellent food. If you think over the ingredients, you will see that they comprise all the different kinds of food we use. I will leave you to hunt up a recipe for that but there is just one recipe I must give you here—that for making bread.

The bread we buy at the baker's is often not by any means the best we could obtain for the price. It is often made as damp as possible, so as to weigh more; and, unfortunately, it often contains substances which have nothing whatever to do with bread. It would be much better if we made most of our bread at home.

Recipe for Making Bread—Ingredients: 2½ lbs. of flour, 1 oz. German yeast, one dessert-spoonful of sugar, one salt-spoonful of salt, 1½ pints of warm water. Mix the sugar, salt, and yeast with the warm water. Strain this into the flour (which should first be well dried); knead it, cover with a cloth and put in a warm place to rise for about half an hour; knead again, and put into a hot oven. If baked in one loaf, it will take an hour; if in two loaves, it will take somewhat less time.

Bread made in this way gets wholesomely dry, but never unpleasantly stale. It is a very bad plan to eat bread when quite fresh.

Intelligent Cookery

When you learn cooking you should never be content with simply following a recipe, or merely doing what you are told. Listen carefully to any **reasons** that are given you for the different methods recommended; for if you know principles and reasons you will be better able to remember details, and you will besides avoid many mistakes which are made by people who have had a good deal of experience in cooking and yet have never found out the nature of the things they use, and are unwilling to learn.

One instance is the mistaken way in which we English people cook potatoes. The protein in a potato is found immediately under the skin, and we usually remove it when we peel a potato. By far the best plan is to wash the potatoes and boil or steam them in their skins. Thus all the best part is kept in. If, however, we choose to peel them we should follow the example of the French cooks, who use the water peeled potatoes have been boiled in for making soups or broths. This water contains a good deal of nourishment from the potato, hence it is very wasteful to throw it away,

Wastefulness

A very common fault in England is that of wastefulness in food. We throw away scraps of bread, of fat, and of vegetables, as well as bacon-rind and bones.

The scraps of bread should be used for puddings or soup, and the fat melted down, clarified and used. The bits of fresh vegetable, as well as fresh apple-peelings and remains of fresh fruit, should go into the soup. The great French cook Soyer, who was called the Napoleon of cooks, used fragments in this way, and so you would also find them used by the economical Frenchwoman, whose cooking, as a rule, is much better than ours.

The bacon-rind can be boiled with lentils, for lentil soup is a very nourishing form of food, and delicious, if well made. As for the bones they should be boiled till they are perfectly white, for only then is all the good taken out of them. The stock so obtained is far better than plain water for making soup or gravy, though of course it should be boiled up daily until used. At night the bones and liquor should be put into separate pans and the stock pot cleaned. This stock will be all the better if we add to it all scraps of meat and the trimmings from joints. We should certainly think more than we do of the value of soup. A good soup is stimulating and warming, and may be also very nourishing. Many a man who on a cold day takes a glass of beer to warm himself would do much better to have a basin of soup or broth. A good housewife will always have a soup-pot going.

Another kind of dish which we might make more use of than we do is the salad. A favourite German salad is made of cold potatoes, oil, vinegar, and pepper; and this is a good way of using up remains of potatoes and other vegetables, especially in summer-time.

To throw away good food because it consists of

fragments is just as foolish as to throw away pence because they are not whole shillings. Wastefulness indicates ignorance or stupidity.

Beverages

We must not forget that what we drink is an important part of our diet.

For allaying thirst the best thing is undoubtedly clean, cool water which has been boiled, and anyone whose taste has not been spoilt will always enjoy a draught of it when thirsty.

Home-made lemonade is a pleasant, wholesome drink, especially in hot weather. It is much to be preferred to bought lemonade, or to beverages made with powders of any kind.

Some kinds of drink are used not so much to allay thirst, as to stimulate or rouse up the nerves to work when they are tired. Such are tea and coffee.

These **stimulants**, as they are called, have no nourishment in them, and it is the greatest mistake to use them as if they were a form of food. They do not give us more strength; they only make us able, for a short time, to use more energetically the strength we already possess.

It is also a mistake to give them to children. When the nerves are young they should never be urged to anything beyond their natural activity. Tired children should have nourishment and rest, and never be excited by stimulants. Warm milk and water is the best drink for their "tea."

What is the use, then, of stimulants? They are chiefly useful as a help to men and women who have their work to do in the world and cannot always lay it aside when they begin to feel weary.

We have already seen that alcohol is frequently called a stimulant—though as a fact it is a narcotic or numbing poison, and, after its first effects have passed off, it always causes fatigue and loss of power; so we will here only speak of tea, coffee, and cocoa. The two things to remember about them are, first, that they should be used with moderation, and secondly that they need to be well made if they are to be good.

Tea

Tea is the non-alcoholic stimulant most used in England; yet many of us have not yet learned to make it well or use it wisely.

It should be made with boiling water, as everyone knows; but, more than that, the water should not have been boiling for some time before it is poured on the tea-leaves; it should have just **freshly come to the boil**. Otherwise all the air dissolved in the water passes off with the steam and the tea tastes flat.

The boiling water draws out of the tea-leaves certain substances which have the effect of rousing the cells of the nervous system to greater activity. This makes us feel refreshed when we have had a good cup of tea.

But it is not a good thing to be always stimulating the nerves in this way, and tea should not be taken more than twice in the day.

The substances which have a pleasant and harmless effect are extracted from the tea-leaves by the water in about three minutes; what passes out after this is an acid which is exceedingly harmful to the stomach, greatly hindering the digestion.

Coffee

It would be a good thing if every English boy and girl learnt how to make coffee. What usually goes by the name of coffee in England is a stuff which no Frenchman or German would condescend to drink. This is because we buy a poor mixture of coffee and chicory, and also because we do not make coffee in the right way. If you want to know how much chicory there is mixed with your coffee, put a small quantity of the mixture in some cold water. If chicory is present, the cold water will become coloured, and the more chicory present the darker the colour.

In countries where coffee is much used, people do not care for alcoholic drinks as they do where it is but little used. Coffee refreshes and stimulates far better than alcohol in any form, and, unless it is taken to a foolish excess, does no harm.

It would therefore be of great advantage to the people of this country if they would cultivate a taste for it; and I will give you the best recipe for making it, that of Soyer, the great cook whom I mentioned just now.

Take a coffee-pot which is fitted with a percolator or filter, as well as a strainer just under the lid. (A metal one may be bought for 1s. 2d.; an earthenware one is somewhat better, but rather more expensive.) Pour some boiling water into it through the filter in order to heat it. Empty this water away, and put into the filter some pure, freshly-ground coffee— taking a dessert-spoonful for each person who is to drink it. Put on the strainer, and then pour boiling water through it into the filter, until the water appears through the holes of the strainer. Then put on the lid, and leave the pot standing in a warm place. In two or three minutes all the water will have run through the filter into the pot below, and you must add some more boiling water, continuing to do so at intervals until the pot below the filter is full. The coffee is then ready to be used, and may be poured off either into cups or into a hot jug or pot.

Do not throw away the coffee-dregs in the filter, but when the pot has been emptied pour some more boiling water over them in the same manner as before. When your pot is full for the second time, pour off its contents and keep them for the next coffee-making. Boiled up again and poured over the fresh coffee in the filter they will prove much better than plain water.

Coffee may be drunk either by itself or with the addition of milk or cream and of sugar. If milk is used it should be boiling, as cold milk with coffee not only makes a poor drink, but also prevents the coffee from having its full stimulating effect.

Cocoa

A drink which is often found very acceptable on a cold day is cocoa. This makes a very good addition to supper in winter-time, and may also be taken with biscuits or bread in the middle of the morning, if the interval between breakfast and dinner is a long one.

It is a mistake to suppose that pure cocoa is specially nourishing, for when used as a drink the quantity taken is too small to contain very much nourishment. Neither does it possess any stimulating properties worth considering. Its chief use is that of a pleasant accompaniment to real food, when cold weather or perhaps long sitting has made one feel chilly.

Most of the cocoa that is sold has starch mixed with it; hence we should be very careful to see that the water or milk with which we make it is absolutely boiling, otherwise we may have a quantity of uncooked starch to drink.

Alcohol

Someone may perhaps ask whether alcohol is a food, nourishing the body in the same way as do starches and fats; and whether, like these foods, it unites with oxygen to give energy and heat, and helps to maintain the fire of life. The answer to this question has been given to us by workers in science. They have proved by many and varied experiments that **alcohol is not a**

food in the practical sense of the word; and although to a certain extent it unites with oxygen, it not only gives us no energy, but by its special action on the nerves and muscles actually takes energy away. So, too, whatever little heat may have been formed by it in the body is entirely lost by its influence on the nerves and blood-vessels, and in the end the body is greatly chilled. In fact, in the Arctic regions people who take alcohol die more quickly than teetotallers.

How to Store Food

Just a word or two must be said as to how to store our food.

The foods which need most care in keeping are meat, fish, butter, and milk. They need this care because they are certain to be attacked by bacteria if neglected.

The place in which they are kept should be dark and cool, but also dry and airy—the more draught there is through it the better. Above all things we must have the larder clean. We cannot be too scrupulous about this, and nowhere in the house will soap and water and some Jeyes' fluid be more useful than here.

If we have no larder the best plan is to store as little food as possible. For such as must be kept in the house it would be a good thing to have a special earthen pan or a box, which should stand on some bricks, covered with a damp cloth, in the coolest place we have. The box should be varnished inside and pierced with holes for ventilation; and if possible it should be fitted with a glass shelf and a glass layer at the bottom. On the glass shelf could be placed the milk and the water boiled for drinking, as well as the butter, while the other eatables could be placed below.

Better still would be the usual safe, with sides of perforated zinc, hung up in a draught. Whatever you have, it should be wiped out every day with water containing Jeyes' fluid, and the shelf in it washed with soap and water.

In hot weather meat should be washed in a little vinegar if it has to be kept till the next day. It is better to buy only so much fish as is required for immediate use, and not attempt to keep it unless it is salted. Butter should stay wrapped in its paper; it is a mistake to expose it to the air. The milk—which should be boiled as soon as it arrives—and the water for drinking should also be kept covered.

By thus taking pains with the storing of our food we shall keep it wholesome and dainty.

Meals and Meal-times

There are, in conclusion, a few simple rules to remember about meals and meal-times. First of all, meals should be regular. Just as we ourselves do better if we take our work in a settled regular order, so do all the organs of our body. They do their work with difficulty if they are made to work irregularly.

We have already seen that great harm is done by bolting food instead of biting it properly. Time spent in having a meal quietly and comfortably is by no means wasted time. Good biting and slow eating allow of a good beginning of digestion; and as the proverb says, "Well begun, is half done." So do not let us hurry and scurry over meals, but eat slowly.

Pleasant talk and laughter are healthful accompaniments to food. If we are vexed or troubled about anything we should not show it at meal-times. Anger and worry hinder the nerves from doing their proper work and prevent the full action of the gastric juice, and thus interfere very much with digestion. The food eaten under such conditions will not nourish us as it ought.

We should have breakfast as soon as possible after getting up, and before doing any hard work. It is a very bad plan to rush straight off to school or to work after a meal—and particularly after breakfast. We should time our meals so as to allow ourselves a short interval of quiet and leisure immediately after them. If there is a long interval between breakfast and the mid-day meal it is a good thing to have a few biscuits, with some milk and hot water or cocoa, or a piece of stale bread and a cup of soup, during the morning. Hunger and exhaustion injure the nerves and weaken the digestion, so that when food is taken after long fasting and exertion the stomach cannot deal with it so well. About three hours is as long as a boy or girl should go without food during the daytime.

On the other hand, we must remember that to be constantly eating is as bad as to go too long without food, and we should not get into the foolish habit of eating sweets and fruit between meals.

Anyone who is going to work hard throughout the day—and especially if the occupation is brain-work—will find it best to have a light mid-day meal, and a good, solid supper—only not too late, for a heavy meal near bedtime is bad. We should never take tea with meat or cheese, as it makes them more difficult to digest by hardening the proteins in them; so that it is better to drink something else at supper—either plain water, lemonade, or cocoa.

Seven o'clock is quite late enough as supper-time for girls and boys, or they will not be ready to go to bed as early as they should.

CHAPTER XII

CLOTHING

"The apparel oft proclaims the man."

— SHAKESPEARE

WHY do we need clothing at all?

You will say, To keep us warm and to protect us from injury and dirt.

Have our brother-animals clothing?

Many of them have scales, fur, feathers or wool, and we have already seen in a previous chapter that all these grow from the skin in the same way as does our own hair. But while our hair, except on the head, affords us no protection, the fur and wool of animals help to keep the temperature of their bodies equable.

Now each animal has its own proper temperature, depending on the rapidity with which the oxygen is sent round its body and so accomplishes that burning of which we learnt in the chapter on Respiration. For the animal to be in good health the temperature must be kept the same. The fur or wool, when the outer air is cold, retains the bodily warmth and prevents it from being lost, whilst when the outer air is warmer than the proper temperature of the body, the fur or wool serves to keep out the heat.

Men have a temperature considerably higher than the average of the surrounding atmosphere in this country—viz., about 98° F. or 37° C.—but they have lost the hairy covering with which, no doubt, their ancestors, the cave-dwellers, were more or less provided. Hence they are obliged to clothe themselves with materials of different kinds.

How it is that Clothes keep us Warm

Before we go on to mention which of these materials are the best, let us pause a moment, and consider more fully how it is that clothes keep us warm.

I daresay most of you on a bitter frosty morning have put your cold hands round your hot tea-cup to warm them. By-and-by, if you held your hand there long enough, it would grow much warmer than before, but, at the same time, you would cease to feel the cup hot. Again, everyone, no doubt, has taken up a bar of brass, or laid his hand round a brass knob, and felt how cold the metal struck and in this case, if the hand holds the brass long enough, it becomes colder than it was, but it ceases to feel the brass to be cold.

In both these cases two objects of unequal temperature are brought into contact with one another, and the hotter one parts with some of its heat to the colder one, to use the ordinary expression, until both are at the same temperature.

This transference of heat by contact is called **con-duction**, and conduction always takes place when two bodies of unequal temperature are brought into contact with one another. You might try to find other examples of this among the things of everyday life; but all substances are not equally ready to part with or to receive heat.

Some substances are extremely quick to respond, if we may so express it; and they are therefore called **good conductors of heat**. Such are metals: you know how soon a metal pot or pan gets hot. Others respond far more slowly, and are therefore called **bad conductors of heat**. Among them are wood, straw, ivory, most liquids, and, above all, air.

Should we Choose Materials that are Good or Bad Conductors?

We have seen that our own natural temperature is higher than that of the surrounding atmosphere— or, at least, nearly always so. Hence we are in some danger of losing our heat, which—by a manner of heat-transference, of which you will doubtless learn more on another occasion—might easily pass, or **radiate**, into space.

How are we to prevent this? If you wish to keep a thing warm you cover it up. And so we cover up our bodies in order to keep in their heat. When covering is interposed between them and the outer air the heat is, as it were, kept within bounds—not wasted on the atmosphere outside the body.

Now, in choosing the material for this covering, which would you judge to be better—a material which is a bad conductor or one which is a good conductor of heat? I think a very little reflection will show you the right answer. If we want the body to keep its heat, we must choose for its covering a material which is a bad conductor.

If we choose a good conductor it will soon respond, as it were, to the heat of the body, and be raised to the same temperature. It will then have to part with its heat to the outer air, much as the body itself would have done if left uncovered; and the body will have to keep making up the loss, and parting with more and more of its own heat.

But if we choose a bad conductor, the stubborn material, keeping more or less its own temperature, despite the heat of the body, will radiate so little heat to the outer air that the body will be able to keep its proper temperature equably.

Wool

The materials for clothing from which we have to make our choice are, of course different fabrics woven of linen, cotton, silk, or wool.

Now, without knowing anything further, we might guess that the last of these would prove particularly useful, because it has already served for the very purpose to which we want to put it. Before it clothes us, wool must have clothed a sheep and kept it warm. It exists, in fact, for no other purpose, whereas linen and cotton are not in the first place designed as clothing for a living creature.

We will therefore consider wool first.

The chief property which makes wool a bad conductor of heat is its fluffiness.

The more fluffy any material is the more air it holds within its substance. Now air, as we saw, is a very bad conductor of heat; in fact, it will let hardly any heat pass through it by conduction. It is mainly the presence of a great deal of air caught in its meshes which makes wool so warm.

We should therefore consider wool as our chief clothing material, the best we have for maintaining the body at an equable temperature. Even in hot weather it is useful; for if it prevents the bodily heat from escaping when the atmosphere is cool, when the atmosphere is too hot it prevents that heat from gaining access to the body better than does cotton or linen.

It is a good thing to have the whole body, except the head and hands, covered with a layer of woollen clothing next the skin. These garments should be stocking-wove, thin in summer and thick in winter. What is worn above them must be determined to a great extent by the age and strength of each person, and the amount of activity and of food which falls to his lot. If we have little exercise and little food, we want more clothing, and *vice versa*.

Woollen clothing next the skin is wholesome in yet another way. It absorbs moisture and allows it to evaporate readily, and thus feels dry itself and keeps the skin dry. Cotton underclothing, on the other hand, absorbs moisture very readily and retains it; hence, after we have perspired freely, when we begin to cool down our cotton clothing is apt to feel chilly and wet. It keeps the skin chilly and wet, too, and this is very likely to give us a cold.

Linen and Cotton

Linen and cotton are useful for outer garments in warm weather, or when one is engaged in any very active employment. They are light in weight; they look nice and fresh when clean; they are easily washed; and, not being fluffy, they catch comparatively little dust or dirt. Hence they are very suitable for outer working clothes, and ought to be used much more than they are in England for that purpose, both by men and women, boys and girls.

On the other hand, it should be remembered that they are not suitable for undergarments. They are good conductors of heat, and so let the bodily warmth escape through them; while, as we saw just now, they retain the perspiration. Hence, neither in summer nor in winter should they be worn next the skin.

Colours

From the point of view of warmth we should perhaps give a thought to colour in choosing our garments. So far as has been at present ascertained, it would seem that dark colours absorb heat more readily than light colours. Hence, in cool weather, if you need a warm garment, black, or some dark shade approaching black, will be found the most suitable colour and pale yellow or white will prove best in hot weather, since this will reflect rather than absorb the heat. It should, however, be remembered that the fluffiness of a material makes more difference to warmth than its colour, on account of the air caught in the fluff. On the whole light colours are more wholesome than dark ones.

Flannelette and Celluloid

Perhaps you will here remind me that there is a fluffy form of cotton material called flannelette, and enquire whether it is good to use.

It is indeed much warmer than cotton woven in the ordinary way; but, since it holds perspiration no less than ordinary cotton stuff, it is not very suitable for wearing next the skin, though it may be worn as a second or outer garment.

It has, however, one very serious disadvantage. Vegetable substances, as a rule, burn more readily than animal substances; and cotton in any form is, of course, far more inflammable than wool. But no cotton fabric is so inflammable as this flannelette. Every year a great number of little children lose their lives by their flannelette nightgowns catching fire.

I should say, then, that anyone who uses flannelette is bound to take every possible precaution against fire, more particularly if that material is used for a baby or a very young child. **A child wearing flannelette should on no account be left in a room without a large guard in front of the fire.**

We may here just mention **celluloid**, often used for combs, collars, cuffs, and other objects, which is a yet more dangerously inflammable substance—so dangerous, in fact, that I doubt whether anyone is justified in using it.

Clothing should Afford Equal Warmth to the Whole Body

To be sensibly clothed very greatly promotes health and comfort. We may say, even more truly, that to be foolishly clothed is injurious to health and growth. Therefore it is worth while to bear in mind the main principles with regard to this.

First of all, our clothing should afford an equal warmth and protection to the whole of the body. It is the greatest mistake to wrap up one part of the body and expose another. We find this mistake most commonly in the clothing of women and girls and young children. Thus you may often see tiny children with their legs exposed to the air, and the lower parts of the body very insufficiently protected, while their shoulders and chests are covered with capes and mufflers, and their heads with hot cloth hoods, caps, or hats. It is very important that the abdomen and thighs should in no case be colder than the rest of the body. Painful, nay, fatal illness is often caused by a chill to these parts and, even if the consequences of exposure are not felt at once, they may affect the whole constitution in after life.

Again, how often we see a girl or woman wearing a warm skirt and above it what is called a "transparent" blouse, in which the upper part, both front and back, consists of nothing but a little flimsy lace or net! Such a garment has well received the further name of the "pneumonia" blouse, for it leaves exposed just that very part of the chest within which are the apices of the lungs. The lungs, as you all know, are very sensitive indeed to chill; and, when chilled, are exceedingly liable to be attacked by the dangerous disease of pneumonia, which you will find mentioned in the list of diseases caused by bacteria.

Exactly how much and how thick clothing each person should wear depends, as we said before, on several considerations but, at any rate, you may make it a rule never to have less clothing over the upper part of the chest than you have over the lower part.

If it is unwise to expose one part of the body more than the rest, it is also unwise to muffle up one part exclusively. Comforters and furs for the neck are common instances of this kind of mistake in clothing.

Worn for the sake of appearance, they are decidedly injurious, for they weaken the throat, and they are also collectors of bacteria and need frequent washing. They should only be used in extreme weather, when all the rest of the body is extra warmly clad and even then, if we can do without them, so much the better.

Shoes and Stockings

We may be otherwise very sensibly dressed and well protected from cold, yet if our feet are shod with shoes and stockings which are too thin, have been allowed to get damp, or are not in good repair, we are very likely indeed to suffer from serious chill. Wet shoes and stockings should be taken off as soon as possible; it is, in fact, better to go barefoot than to keep damp things on one's feet. Every child who goes to school should keep at the school-house a pair of shoes and stockings, so that if, by any chance, the feet have got wet in the walk to school, there may be dry things ready to put on.

Headgear

The one part of the body which needs to be kept cool rather than warm is the head. Except in extremes of heat and cold, hats and caps are chiefly useful as a shade to the eyes and a protection from dust, and we might go bareheaded with advantage most days of the year.

The head should always have the air playing freely

round it, and therefore bonnets which cover up the whole head and the ears should be avoided, especially as they tend to spoil the hearing. The silk top-hats and bowlers worn by boys and men also prevent proper ventilation, as well as make the head too hot.

Provided it is light, well ventilated, and comfortable it does not much matter what kind of hat you wear, except when the sun is very hot. At such a time there is danger of sunstroke, and it is wise to wear some kind of white or light-coloured covering on the head, so that the hot rays may be reflected off before they reach the head. It is also important to have a hat with a wide brim which will shade the nape of the neck, for this part is very liable to sunstroke. The pith helmet, white, light in weight, and coming right down to the neck, is one of the best things to wear in hot summer weather. Equally useful is a cotton (such as galatea) covering for the hat, with a flap behind over the back of the neck.

Warmth during Sleep

I have just one more thing to mention in connection with clothing and warmth, and that is the necessity for being kept warm when asleep. Grown-up people very commonly sleep at night under too much bed-clothing rather than too little; but young children are often not sufficiently cared for in this respect. I do not mean that they have not enough bed-clothes, but that they often throw them off, and are not always covered up again. To sleep more or less uncovered is very bad for them, and little children need watching at night to prevent this. It is equally important to cover up a child when sleeping in the day-time—more especially if asleep in a perambulator in the open air. The covering used should be a woollen one, and not heavy.

Clothing should be Loose and Easy

In the next place, clothing should be loose and easy. Do you know how to find out whether your clothes are loose enough? Unbutton your coat, or waistcoat, or bodice—whatever you may be wearing—and unfasten any bands. Then lie down on some flat surface, stretch out your arms horizontally, as wide as they will go, and, while you remain in this position, let some friend come and try to button your clothes up. If they can be fastened easily, then they are of the right size; if they will not meet, they are too tight. The clothes of very few people, whether men or women, boys or girls, will stand the test; there is great need of giving some attention to this matter.

We have already seen that tight clothing compresses important organs of the body in a very injurious way. In growing children it may interfere with the proper shape and position of the bones, and it will make it impossible for them to acquire the habit of deep breathing. Tight clothes are bad for the circulation, for the skin, and for the muscles. The muscles of a woman's back are often weak merely because she holds herself up by means of bits of steel and whalebone, instead of by the support with which Nature has provided her. It is quite an error to suppose this is necessary, for the great majority of the women of the world do not wear stays. The women of India, China, and Japan, who have never enclosed themselves in this sort of cage, are quite as graceful and strong and active as the women of Western nations.

Besides taking care that our clothes are loose enough over the trunk, with plenty of room for the chest, with no tight band pressing in the region of the waist, we should remember that tight collars, tight garters, and tight shoes are very harmful.

The stiff linen collars which little boys are made to wear are a most unfortunate whim of fashion. Their use entails much unnecessary expenditure of time and money in washing, starching and ironing. A clean collar is not the same thing as a clean boy. One may often see the poor children wriggling their heads in discomfort—and they are sometimes enduring more than discomfort, for the collar, pressing on the blood-vessels which go to the head, causes headache and a feeling of being throttled. It will be a good thing when tight collars of all kinds, whether worn by little boys, by soldiers, or by any other persons, go out of fashion; and we can do something towards this end by leaving them off ourselves. After all, sailors do not wear them; and you will not see anywhere a neater, more active, and manly appearance than is presented by the men who serve in our Navy.

Tight garters interfere with the movement of the blood in the veins of the leg, and may often cause serious injury; whilst tight boots and shoes, and those with pointed toes, deform the foot and spoil the walk.

While we are speaking of shoes, we may as well mention the fact that high heels are bad for the foot, for the knee, and for the spine, since they force all the joints into unnatural positions, alter the proper balance of the body, and quite spoil the arch of the instep by throwing the weight on the toes.

Light in Weight

Thirdly, it is important to remember that clothing should be as light in weight as we can get it without giving up necessary warmth.

If you were to pack up to send by post the clothes which a girl or boy ordinarily wears at one time, you would probably be astonished to find how much your parcel weighed.

To lift and carry weight requires energy, and energy spent in dragging about superfluous clothing is spent in pure waste. What is hardly felt, even as an inconvenience, by a strong person may be very tiring to a weak one; and many small children are made to endure quite unnecessary fatigue by being dressed in heavy coats or pelisses, or in heavy boots. These last sometimes turn the toes under and spoil the growth of the foot. It may be said that as a general rule the boots of little boys are heavier than they ought to be.

When we are choosing clothing we should always decide on the lightest material or garment out of the number of otherwise suitable ones.

How the weight of the clothing is distributed over the body is also a matter to be considered. The shoulders and the waist are the two places from which we mostly suspend our garments, and it is the former which should carry the principal weight.

And Clean

Finally, clothing should be clean. If you look back for one moment at the chapter on the skin I think you will realize that to wear unwashed and unaired clothing day after day is a most unwholesome practice.

It seems scarcely necessary to say any more about the washing of under-garments; we are all well aware of the importance of this. But do we sufficiently consider that our outer garments want cleaning and washing also? The perspiration, and the various matters thrown off by the skin, do not all stop in the first layer of clothing they come to; a great part of them penetrates into every garment we wear, though we may not perceive it. Suits and dresses that have been worn year in year out without washing or cleaning become very dirty indeed, so dirty that if their wearers could see all that is held fast in them they would be utterly disgusted.

The coats and trousers worn by men and boys—even by well-to-do persons otherwise careful about cleanliness—are particularly liable to become receptacles of this kind of dirt, as anyone who has a nose may discover. It is not creditable to the English workman that his presence is so often disagreeable, especially as this is by no means one of the things that cannot be helped. American working men, for instance, and also the Japanese, are far more cleanly.

Cloth clothes and corduroys are very difficult and tiresome to wash, but they get much less dirty if they are used with linings which can be taken out and washed easily and frequently.

In Japan, in preparation for every season, the clothes which are to be worn again are all taken to pieces, thoroughly washed out, and then sewn up again. Some such practice as this would be a good thing for us also; and it would probably lead to our having lighter and better clothes, at least for summer wear.

The worst instance of uncleanliness commonly to be observed in women's clothes is that of the trailing skirt. Anyone who has even a little knowledge or a little good taste must surely feel sickened at the thought of the filth swept up from the streets by such a garment. Disease germs of all kinds must necessarily cling to it—more especially so long as the disgusting habit of spitting still prevails. Its wearer carries them with her into every place she enters, whether it be church, or shop, or a friend's house, or her own bedroom, or perhaps a home full of little children.

And may be Pretty

You must not suppose that clothing, in order to be sensible, must no longer be pretty. Get a book which shows you the costumes of different nations, and you will see many, far more becoming than those we wear, which are also practical and healthful—the women's skirts being quite short and their waists the right size round.

The most beautiful clothing is that which is most suitable to the wearer and to his or her requirements, which is kept clean and fresh, delighting the eye with well-chosen colour, and leaving the body free for graceful and active movement.

The Hair

Since, among girls and women at any rate, the hair is considered as important a part of the personal appearance as the dress, we have reserved what there is to say about it for this place.

It goes without saying that the hair ought to be kept clean. It should be carefully brushed for at least five or ten minutes every day, and occasionally washed. I need not remind my readers that neglected and dirty hair is not only very disagreeable to see, but may easily become extremely offensive in other ways.

But besides keeping the hair and the head clean I think that girls and women should apply their commonsense to the arrangement of their hair more than many of them do. On an ordinary week-day, when they are busy at work, whether it be at school or in the house, in a shop, or in a factory, it is very unsuitable for girls to have their hair flying loose, or arranged in a fluffy mass over the forehead. Just as working clothes should be plain, neat, close-fitting, and not of a kind to catch dust and dirt, so a girl who is really dainty and careful about her appearance will choose to have her hair neatly and closely arranged while at work. On high days and holidays perhaps she will alter her fashion a little; but even on these she will not sacrifice the natural beauty of her hair in order to obtain a curling fringe or artificial waves.

Curling-irons and curling-pins are very injurious things; they make the hair brittle and spoil its growth. Curling the hair is a fashion which goes far back to savage times, when a much-befrizzed head, stuck over with various oddments, was considered a mark of dignity.

CHAPTER XIII

THE HOME

*"What you do not like when done to yourself,
do not do to others."*

— CONFUCIUS, B.C. 550

WHILE learning about the different parts of our bodies we often turned to our fellow-animals to see how far we resembled them. We discovered that we are like them in many things, and what is true in this respect of the body of man is also true of his home.

The making of a home and the love of home go back to a time before the first men existed, and just as, by studying the lowly creatures around us, we may see something of the beginning of our bodily organs, so we may see what was the beginning of our human homes by observing those of animals.

Not all animals have homes. Many which wander about in herds feed on the open pastures, and sleep there without shelter.

Nor do all the animals which make homes inhabit them the whole year round. Thus birds may have nests only in spring and summer: when the young have flown the nests are deserted.

248

The first homes were like nests in this respect. They were merely quiet hiding-places for the young to stay in whilst they were frail and small, where the mother might feed the little ones without fear of enemies. By degrees many of them came to be used as permanent dwelling-places and storehouses for food, while some animals settled together in colonies, or in a single great home like that of the ants and the bees.

The earliest and simplest animal homes are burrows, such as are inhabited by worms; by various crabs and beetles and spiders; by rabbits, foxes, moles, and other mammals. Perhaps one of the most curious burrows is that of the polar bear, which is dug out under the ice. Though it appears to us a very cold and miserable home, its owner finds it warm and comfortable.

A rather more advanced kind of dwelling is made by weaving together leaves, rushes, tiny twigs, bits of wool and other such materials. The nests of spiders, birds, squirrels, mice, and many other animals are made in this way, and we may observe all degrees of skill in their construction, from the rough nest of the magpie to the dainty home of the tailor-bird. Many fish make nests of sea-weed or water-weed; while the larger apes make shelters for themselves in trees in much the same manner.

Next there are homes made by plastering clay over twigs, or constructed out of some material resembling clay. These approach nearest to our own homes; and perhaps the best instances of them are the combs of bees, the lodges of beavers, and the great termite mounds.

Many creatures are very careful of their homes. Among the flesh-eating animals great pains are taken to keep the den and the cubs clean, so that no smell may betray where they are. The cleverest and most diligent of all, however, are the ants and the bees, who surpass many human communities in this respect.

The Growth of the Home

Men have made for themselves homes as various as those of animals. The earliest men lived in caves, much like burrows, and these old cave-dwellings have been found in most parts of the world, still containing the bones of the people who occupied them, as well as the bones of dogs and of wild animals killed in hunting. Very few, even of the most savage peoples, now live in caves.

Better than these are the homes built of boughs, and covered with bark or woven mats, forming a wigwam or a hut (Figure 36). In many places, where the hut-builders had herds of cattle, they used skins to cover the boughs or poles, and thus formed a tent. Great numbers of different tribes, living in very different parts of the world, made dwellings of this kind. They were easy to make and easy to move, and they served well for people who wandered from one place to another seeking water and fresh pasture for cattle. You will say such homes as these must have afforded but very slight shelter. True; among the more wretched savages the hut did little more than serve as a screen to keep their fire from being blown out. But we must remember that

FIGURE 36 — PRIMITIVE MAN AT HOME

these savages, like the gipsies of the present day, lived mostly in the open air, and though, no doubt, they suffered in many ways, they did not require shelter as much as we do.

These huts and tents came by degrees to be made more and more skillfully. Some of the blacks in Africa still make bee-hive huts which are very beautiful in their way, and show us what the ancient hut-building must have been at its best.

Such dwellings as these could only be made of flexible materials; and the next stage takes us to the people who gave up these and first made proper houses, built of wood. The Malay houses, which may be seen in the islands of the Indian Archipelago, are examples of the first work done by uncivilized people in this way. These dwellings are of different designs, are ornamented, and have more than one room.

When houses were thus made permanent structures, it became a great misfortune to have them destroyed by any accident, or taken by enemies; and the desire for protection led to several new developments. Many people built their houses on piles, and often raised them to a considerable height from the ground (Figure 37). This allowed water to run away underneath them, and kept off the inroads of destructive animals, as well as made it more difficult for an enemy to force his way in. In fact, these raised habitations were looked upon as so safe that some tribes took to making their houses in trees.

Then, again, other tribes drove tree-trunks, or piles,

FIGURE 37 — PILE-DWELLINGS

into the ground a little way out from the shore of a lake or a river, and built their homes upon them over the water. The remains of such lake-dwellings have been found in England and in the lakes of Switzerland, whilst in New Guinea and elsewhere there are many fishing villages constructed on the same plan to this day. No doubt protection from wild beasts and enemies was the first object in making a home of this fashion; but pile-building by the water-side has been continued without any such necessity, as you may see in the cities of Venice, Amsterdam, and St. Petersburg, which are built on piles, though the houses are not all of wood as were those of the original pile-builders.

Lastly, we must mention houses and huts made with wood plastered over with clay. Such were made by the ancient Britons in our own island, as well as by many other peoples in many other countries. It is chiefly by greater and greater improvements in this kind of dwelling, combined after a time with the use of stones and of clay baked into bricks, that we have arrived at the houses and the greater buildings used by civilised peoples at the present day.

Wooden houses are very common in some parts of the Continent and also in America; but we seldom see them in England. They are warm and comfortable in many ways; but are, of course, easily destroyed by fire.

Iron frameworks are now often used in place of wood, especially in those huge erections many storeys high seen in American cities, which have been nicknamed "skyscrapers."

The Needs of Modern Homes

As men passed from barbarism to civilization, they began to engage in many employments which could not well be carried on in the open air.

In our own part of the world we find great numbers of people who spend most of their lives indoors, and some who hardly go out at all. This makes it the more important that all homes should be healthy, and that everyone should know how to make and keep them so.

Now in what we learnt about the body we saw that to be healthy it needs sunlight and air; and we saw further that our enemies the bacteria of disease flourish most amid damp, darkness and dirt. Bearing this in mind, can you tell me what we ought to aim at, and what we ought to avoid in building or choosing a house?

Perhaps someone will suggest that we must avoid damp. That is a good answer. What we want first of all is a dry soil, and next we want dry foundations and floors and dry walls.

The Best Soils for Houses

There are some soils so loosely held together that they let water through very easily; there are others which, being much more compact, only suffer it to penetrate them very slowly and therefore hold it a long time. If you take three flower-pots and half fill them, one with sand, one with gravel, and one with clay, you will soon discover which soil holds the water longest. It will rush through the sand and the gravel almost immediately, but will lie on the clay for some time before it even soaks in.

Which kind of soil would you choose to build your house upon? The sand, you will answer, or the gravel. Perfectly right; yet remember one thing. In many places a shallow layer of sand or gravel lies upon a bed of clay. The clay acts like a cup, and holds up the water in the porous soil above. This makes a very bad site for a house; therefore examine the gravel well before you build, and make sure that it goes deep enough.

Foundations

However dry the ground may be we must not build immediately upon it. A firm layer of concrete at least half-a-foot thick should cover the whole of the area on which our house stands. The reason for this is the fact that all soil contains air, and this ground-air is laden with bacteria,—very often with those most injurious to us. Now when the air within the house becomes warm and rises, this ground-air will rush in to take its place, and may bring with it the germs of consumption, diphtheria, or some other dangerous disease—unless we have laid down a good barrier of concrete to prevent this.

If the soil is damp we may take the extra precaution of having pipes laid under the foundations of our house. These pipes should be unglazed and porous—such as are used in the fields to drain water into ditches; and they should not empty into a sewer, but into a river or a ditch. By this means much of the water in the soil will be collected and drawn away, and the foundations will be kept the drier.

Walls

Next we must consider the walls of our house. They will probably be either of brick or of stone; and we should take care that the brick or the stone is the hardest of its kind, for both are in any case porous, and rain may soak through them. Brick houses are now built with double walls which have an air-space between them, so that moisture from without cannot make its way into the interior. Air being, as we said, a bad conductor of heat, this kind of wall keeps a house warm. If rain soaks in through a solid wall the only thing to do is to put on a facing of cement or tiles.

But however safe from rain we have made our building, we shall still be troubled with damp unless we can prevent the moisture in the soil from rising into the walls.

If you wish to see exactly what happens you have only to get three or four common red bricks and a pan with a little water in it. Lay a brick in the pan, and by slow degrees the water will soak into it and saturate it. Then place another brick upon the first, and you will see the water rise into that also. If you put a third brick upon the second the water will again rise, and will continue to do so as long as you choose to go on piling bricks and supplying sufficient water. Thus it is that moisture from a damp soil creeps up our walls.

But if you obtain a glazed brick and lay it on No. 3, and then put a fourth ordinary brick on the top, you will find No. 4 remains dry, The water is stopped by the glaze. You can now tell me how to prevent our walls from getting damp. You will say at once, Lay a row of these glazed bricks in the walls a little above the surface of the ground.

Such a row, called a damp-proof course, may be seen in most newly-built houses. The glazed bricks are usually perforated from side to side, as air makes the protection yet more complete.

We should be careful not to let the soil come into contact with the bricks above the damp-proof course, as thereby the protection is rendered useless. It is also much better to keep the part of the walls which goes below the surface from such contact, for moisture soaking through will make the lowest part of the house chill and unwholesome. The soil should be faced with a layer of bricks at a distance of an inch or two from the wall, and the space thus made should be covered in. There are preparations of silicate known as "water-glass," which are soluble in hot water, and can be put on walls which are damp. When dried they become perfectly hard, and prevent any further oozing out of moisture. "Water-glass" is much used in Germany, and should be better known in this country.

Roof

What roof would you choose for your house? There are roofs of slate, of tiles, of thatch, of lead, and of one or two other materials less often used. Lead is dear and heavy; thatch is damp and apt to catch fire and harbour insects; slate is light, but it is hot in summer and cold in winter. You will be wisest, on the whole, in choosing the pretty red tiles which give the gabled roofs of so many old towns their beautiful colouring.

Woodwork

When our walls are rising and we are putting in the woodwork of our house we should be careful to see that well-seasoned wood is used. Green wood shrinks, as you know, and in the cracks thus made in floors or window-frames or doors dust collects and draughts whistle, while the windows and doors constructed of such wood often rattle and shake in a very maddening way. This shrinking is particularly undesirable in floors, as there most dirt will collect; and if you live in a house where the boards gape asunder you should make a point of filling the spaces with strips of wood. The wood used for floors should be as hard as possible, for the softer kinds make much more dust.

Aspect

A house may be perfectly dry, yet if it lacks sunlight and air it will not be healthy. So when we are choosing or building a house to live in we should always consider its aspect. If we can get plenty of sunshine we may well put up with many little inconveniences. We should aim at having a house where the sun looks into all the rooms at some time or other of the day.

If your largest and best room looks towards the north away from the sun, and you have a back room that faces the south and the sunshine, you should use the latter most.

Air-space

Dwellers in the country enjoy one immense advantage over dwellers in towns, and that is the air space they can have round their homes. But though, in towns, we cannot all live in detached houses round which the air can play freely, yet we ought, at any rate, to have open space at the front and back, so that a current of air can sweep right through. Back-to-back houses ought never to be built, and you should never live in such a one if you can by any possibility avoid it. The harmfulness of such dwellings cannot be exaggerated.

Some people whose houses are in themselves pleasant and comfortable make the great mistake of not using them. They will keep a "best" sitting-room shut up from one week to another while the whole family crowds together in the kitchen where the meals are cooked and eaten. Now it is an excellent thing to change from one room to another during the day, so that one may be well aired while the other is occupied. In towns, at any rate, there are comparatively few people who have even as much air-space as they need, and none have more than is necessary. So keep your rooms for use and not for show.

How much fresh air does each person want? Roughly about 3,000 cubic feet every hour. Suppose four persons are sitting in a room twelve feet long, ten feet wide, and ten feet high. They require to have the air completely changed ten times in the course of an hour. This is equally necessary whether the persons are children or grown up. Many of the health troubles of children are caused or much increased by breathing impure air in a shut-up room. When people are sitting together by gaslight or lamp-light even more air must be supplied, for the light in burning consumes oxygen and gives off carbon dioxide, as you know. An ordinary gas-burner counts as rather more than equal to a person and a half.

Our need of fresh air is as great by night as by day, and we should never have our windows quite shut at night. If we suppose that you spend eight hours in bed, you would want a room thirty feet wide, fifty feet long, and sixteen feet high all to yourself to supply you with the proper amount of air. Since most of us can hardly hope ever to have such a bedroom as that, we must let plenty of air into our smaller room, and besides opening the window we must be sure that the chimney is not blocked. The reason for this is that we must have two openings if we wish to air a room properly—one by which the fresh air may enter, the other for the escape of the used-up air. This seems to be forgotten by many people.

Ventilation

At least once a day, even in bad weather, all the windows should be thrown wide open and the house aired right through. In fine summer weather there is no reason why any windows should be shut, except perhaps in extreme heat or when dust is beating straight upon them. After breakfast is the best time for this airing if it has to be temporary, and in an ordinary house it should last fifteen minutes at the very least.

Bedroom windows should stay open all day; and if for any reason you cannot keep open the windows of the room you are sitting in you must be all the more careful to open them wide every moment it is unoccupied. A person who begins young enough can, if he is ordinarily strong, train himself to disregard draughts, but this experiment should not be tried with old people. Still it must not be forgotten that the aged require plenty of fresh air, and they should be given a cosy corner or some extra clothing rather than be allowed to sit in an unventilated room.

When a room is empty and being aired a sash-window should be open at the top and bottom; when the room is occupied the window should be open at the top. By this means the air entering from outside is mingled with warm air that rises to the ceiling, and a cold draught is avoided. A very good method of ventilation was invented by Dr. Hinckes-Bird for use in sash-windows (Figure 38). A solid block of wood going the whole width of the window is placed under the lower sash. It should be about two inches in width, and will thus raise the lower sash that much above the lower bar of the upper sash. Through the space made by this means the air comes in on an upward current, and so no draught is felt.

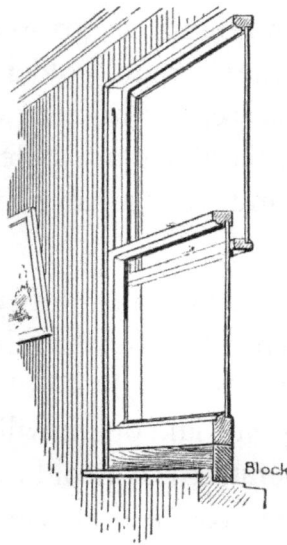

FIGURE 38 — *Method of ventilating sash windows by inserting a block of wood beneath the lower sash, leaving a space between the upper and lower sashes.*

There are many other inventions in the way of ventilators, and you might try to find out some of them by inquiring among your grown-up friends. The best of all, however, is the open window; and if you once get the taste for fresh air you will not want much persuasion to have recourse to that.

Temperature

A chilly room is uncomfortable, and so is an over-heated one, while both are bad for health, and especially the latter. So the sensible manager of a house will take some thought about the warming of the rooms.

Now this is a matter in which it is a great mistake to go by one's own sensations, for some people feel, as we say, much warmer or much colder than others do at the same temperature, and nothing is more common than to see a number of persons suffering because one or two are selfish and unreasonable about this question of heat or cold.

The best way to avoid such difficulties is to have a thermometer and regulate the warmth of the room by it. A thermometer may be bought for ninepence, and you will find it money well laid out. It will tell you not only whether the temperature is high or low enough, but also how nearly equable you keep it. This is an important point in the care of the very young, of the aged, and of those who are delicate, for to them sudden rises and falls of temperature may be very hurtful.

From 60° F. to 65° F. is the right general warmth for a sitting-room. A place where active work is being done may be somewhat cooler, as also the bedroom of one who is in ordinary health. The more people there are in the room or the house the smaller fire will you need and the more air.

A slight fall of the general temperature is better met by wearing a little extra clothing than by heating up the rooms. Those of us who are strong and well fed should aim at requiring even this as little as possible, for during their vigorous years men and women ought to be able to endure a considerable increase of heat or cold without discomfort. In this, as in many other things, we may learn of the Japanese.

We English people are terribly wasteful in our methods of warming. It has been calculated that five-eighths of the heat from our ordinary open grates goes up the chimney. We are thus burning more than half our coal to no better purpose than to make the air around our house black and sooty, and to draw nearer the time when our coal-supply will be exhausted. Moreover, this method of warming gives the least equability of temperature and warms the smallest area, whilst it makes a great amount of work by the dirt and dust it causes.

Let me remind you that wastefulness shows ignorance or stupidity.

A great deal of heat might be saved if all chimneys were placed in the middle of the house instead of against outside walls as they usually are. You know how warm the wall becomes around the kitchen fire. There is no sense in squandering half that warmth on the outer air. If you ever have to plan or build a house, remember to put your chimney-stack in the very middle of it.

Yet another improvement, is to have the back of the fireplace made of fire-clay and sloped forwards over the fire. Much of the heat which would otherwise be lost up the chimney is by this means radiated into the room.

Stoves

The Germans heat their houses very much more economically than we do. They use stoves lined with fire-brick and covered with tiles. These stoves are often very pretty both in design and in colouring, and they may have shelves arranged at the sides for drying or keeping things warm.

Two objections are very commonly made to the use of stoves: first, that they make the air of the room feel so dry; and secondly, that they cannot serve as a means of ventilation like the open fireplace.

The first of these objections may be met by placing on the stove an iron pot or basin filled with water, which should be regularly renewed as it evaporates.

With regard to the second, stoves have been invented which supply a room with fresh and warm air better than does the open fireplace, which merely creates a current of air from under the doors or through the windows towards and up the chimney. The best kind of stove is enclosed in a sort of iron covering much larger than itself. This forms an air-chamber, which is connected with the outer air by a pipe under the floor. The hot air in this air-chamber rises into the room through a grating in the top of the iron cover, drawing fresh cold air up through the pipe to be warmed and sent out in the same way. Thus a supply of air, which is both warm and fresh, is constantly rising into the room.

The stove should be made of wrought iron—not of cast iron, and should be covered outside with tiles. It should be lined with fire-clay. If care is not taken about these points, or if a defective stove is used, poisonous gases produced by the burning of coal and coke will escape into the room.

A good stove of this sort, burning in a hall or passage, will often be found enough to warm a whole house, and will do so in a very economical and satisfactory manner.

Gas fires need the same precaution as a stove, for they, too, cause the air to feel very dry; but if water is allowed to evaporate into the room they are wholesome and useful, being easily regulated and clean. Of course, escape of the gas must be carefully guarded against.

Drainage

One of the most important points about the management of a house is undoubtedly that of getting rid of the refuse, and of the waste matter, or **excreta**, of our own bodies.

To do this effectively requires constant and steady care and some knowledge both of the dangers we are to guard against and the apparatus we are to use.

In towns and in many country houses excreta and liquid refuse are carried away from the house by water drainage. That is to say, each house has attached to it a system of pipes which empty either into a cesspool prepared in the ground or else into another much larger system of pipes, which collects the waste from different parts of a town and carries it away. What becomes of it then is a question which does not concern us here; it is with the pipes belonging to each house that we have to do.

Now the matter which these pipes carry off is exceedingly dangerous to health, and must on no account be allowed to leak out into the open. Therefore, the first things to make sure of are that the drainpipes are properly made of stoneware and have no flaw in them and also that where one pipe fits into another the joint is well cemented and water-tight. If you have any reason to suppose that your drains are leaking you should communicate with the sanitary authority of the place in which you live, in order that they may be tested. This is done by filling the whole system of pipes either with smoke or with water, when the rising of smoke through any aperture, or the leaking out of the water, shows that the pipes are not sound. The water test is the severer and therefore the more satisfactory, of the two.

Next it is necessary that the noxious matter in the drains be got rid of quickly; hence drain-pipes should go straight down the wall of a house, and when they enter the ground should be laid on a bed of concrete and on a fairly steep slope, so that whatever is sent down them may pass along rapidly. The course of a drain-pipe should be as regular and straight as possible. There must be no sharp corners or deep curves. If a bend is necessary it must be a very gradual one.

They should never run inside a house nor yet under any part of it, but should lead at once from the place where they receive the refuse or excreta, out into the open air. This is exceedingly important, for much illness and many deaths have been caused by drainpipes being laid within the walls of a house or under the rooms. Anyone whose house is in this condition should consult the sanitary authority on the subject and get it altered.

Trapping and Ventilation of Pipes

But though the pipes are sound, have a good fall, and run outside the house, we shall yet be in a very great danger if they are not also properly trapped and ventilated. I must explain what this means.

The entire system of pipes, both the part belonging to each house and that belonging to the town or village as a whole, is full of air. With this air are mingled foul gases and bacteria from the excreta and the refuse sent into the drains. Now gas is a substance which moves and expands in any direction as far as there is room for it. Therefore, though the solid or liquid matters themselves are got rid of, the gases from them rise and pass up through the pipes wherever they can, and make their way into the house again. This sewer-gas is one of the most deadly of all our enemies, bringing with it terrible possibilities of disease, and we must keep it out at all costs.

Now, except under extraordinary pressure, the gas will not pass rapidly through water, but will only be slowly absorbed by it and diffused through it. Therefore, at three places at least, in the course of the drain-pipe from the house to the sewer, we must have a deep bend made in the pipe, so that when we send water down into the drain some of it may remain standing in the bend and act as a seal or barrier against the gas. The more often this water is renewed the safer is the barrier. Such a bend, filled with water, is called a **trap**. The most important points to trap are first the bit of pipe immediately beneath the pan or sink within the house, secondly the place where the pipe from the house joins the drain laid in the earth, and thirdly the place where the drain joins the sewer.

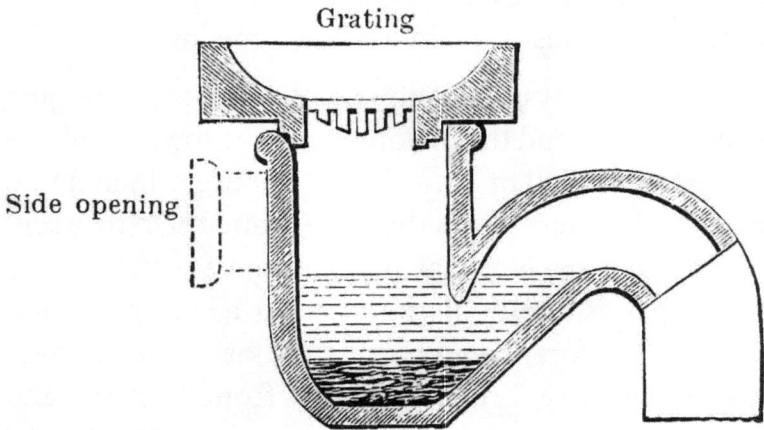

FIGURE 39 — YARD GULLY

The waste-pipe discharges through a side opening
below the grating, and above the water which acts as a trap.

The pipe from a sink should discharge into the open air over a gully, and the hole of the gully should be a little way out beyond the opening of the pipe. Then any gas that may rise from the gully will not ascend the sink-pipe and enter the house, but will diffuse into the open air. Another good form of gully is that shown in Figure 39.

The traps for the pipes carrying excreta, and also that immediately below the sink should be some kind of syphon-trap (Figure 40); those for sinks and baths where the waste joins the drain should be **gully-traps**. You should look carefully at the illustrations, and should compare the syphon-trap with the old-fashioned bell-trap (Figure 41). This latter is a very bad form of trap, and should no longer be used anywhere, as poisonous gases pass through it easily.

Now, no doubt some intelligent reader will say, Yes, but the gas in the pipes must surely go somewhere; otherwise the pressure will be greater and greater and will force it through the trap. To prevent this we have the **ventilating shaft**, and also an **open grating** for ventilation in the ground between the house-drain and the main sewer. The ventilating shaft is a straight pipe carried up from the drains into the air, and open at the top. It should on no account be shorter than the house to which it belongs or than neighbouring houses, as the foul gases escaping from the top of it may enter at windows and even saturate walls. Rainwater pipes should never be used for this purpose.

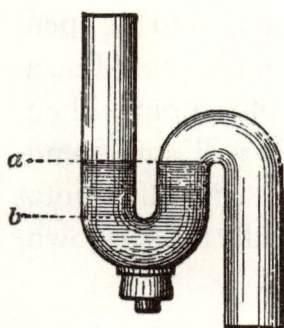

FIGURE 40 — SYPHON TRAP

*The water between **a** and **b** acts as a seal against the sewer-gas.*

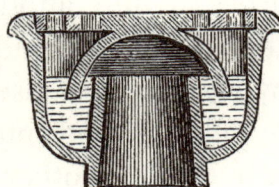

FIGURE 41 — OLD BELL-TRAP

This is defective, because there is not enough depth of water to act as a seal, and because it readily becomes choked with grease.

Use of Earth and Ashes

In some houses, both in towns and in the country, there is no water laid on, and no drainage system. A pail is usually arranged to receive the excreta. It is exceedingly important that this should be emptied every day, and that ashes or earth should be thrown into it whenever it has been used. The contents of such a pail are a valuable manure; and this method of getting rid of excreta is a very healthy one, provided only it is conducted with reasonable care.

Cleanliness

The most perfect drainage system in the world most perfectly carried out will, however, be of no use to a house unless the inmates are clean and careful. Never throw bits of rag, thick paper, hair, matches, flower-stalks or any other rubbish down your drains, since these will stop up the pipe. Burn all the rubbish you possibly can, for this is a more healthy way of disposing of it than leaving it in a dust-bin for the dustmen to clear away.

Never pour fat down your sink, for this makes the pipe foul and causes a particularly noxious smell very difficult to get rid of.

Send plenty of clean water, or water with some disinfectant in it, down your drains from time to time, especially if your household is a large one.

A strong solution of washing-soda will help to keep your sink clean; but better still are tidy ways in washing up plates and dishes. No fragments of any kind should be suffered in the sink at all; they should be scraped into a bit of paper, screwed up and put at the back of the fire—when it is burning hottest—and well covered with ashes or a damp mixture of small coal and coke. Pieces of waste paper can be used for wiping greasy knives and plates before they are washed. This will effect economy in washing. The cloths, mops, and brushes we use at the sink should all be kept scrupulously clean. If there is any smell from them after washing up is over, they are not clean.

We must remember as we stand at the sink, washing our pots and pans, that we stand between our household and its invisible enemies.

Water

Besides the system of pipes, which carry off waste matter, the greater number of houses are now furnished with another set of pipes which convey the water-supply.

This water may be pumped up from a well belonging to a house, or it may be part of the general water-supply of a town, derived from springs or a river, perhaps even from a lake or the streams of a valley many miles away.

When the water is drawn from a well, great care should be taken to prevent any of the drainage from the soil finding its way into the well. The neighbourhood of a cesspool is very dangerous, more especially if the cesspool and the well are so situated with regard to one another that the fall of the ground is from the former towards the latter. Even if the fall is the other way, the water of a well will be polluted by a cesspool near it if the well is very low. These dangers may be avoided by sinking the well at a proper distance from any cesspool and by constructing it with great care. The sides should be built of brickwork lined with a cement which will not allow of the passage of water; and the mouth should be covered over. The neighbourhood of pig-styes, manure-heaps, and stables is also dangerous.

It is a mistake to suppose that because water is bright, sparkling, and pleasant to the taste it is therefore pure. Some of the most dangerous water has this appearance.

When the water for the house is supplied by

waterworks, the chief points for the householder to attend to are the position of his storage-cistern, its cleanliness, and the material of which it is made.

The best materials are stoneware, galvanized iron, or slate, as these make no difference to the water. The cistern should be covered over, and should be cleaned out about four times every year. It should be placed in an airy and light part of the house, and should have no communication with the drainage system. This last point is the most important of all for if any pipe from any part of the drainage system of the house goes to the water-cistern there will be very great danger of foul air finding its way into the water-supply.

Nowhere ought these two systems of pipes to run near one another or communicate; the water necessary for flushing the drains should be sent into a separate flushing-cistern. In houses where there is no storage-cistern and water is drawn direct from the main this precaution is no less necessary. If you have no proper flushing-cistern, but have to flush your drains direct from the water-supply of the house, you should ask the advice of the sanitary authority about this.

We must mention once again that **water should be boiled before it is used for drinking**. This will not only render it safe from impurities which cause disease, but will soften water that is too hard by causing the carbonate of lime in it to sink to the bottom as a solid deposit.

I will here give you a test by which you may discover whether the water supplied to your house is pure. You must not suppose that it is a complete test, for that would be too difficult and complicated for you to try but it will be of service in detecting some of the worst kinds of impurity.

Make a solution of permanganate of potash. Pour a little of the solution into a glass of water, just sufficient to give the water a very faint pink tinge. Cover the glass, and let it stand for half an hour. If the pink colour has not become brown, or discoloured in any way, the water may be considered pure.

Rooms Should be Well Lighted

The rooms where we sit together, where we have our meals, where we sleep, these are what we see with the mind's eye when we speak of home and when you plan what you will do in a home of your own these are the parts of the house you think most about. It is now time to consider how we should furnish and arrange them, that they may be as healthy as possible.

First of all, every room in a house ought to be as cheerful as we can make it. How shall we ensure this? What is the best thing we can have to brighten everything up, and make our home look joyous and gay?

The best thing we can have is light. A bare, clean room full of light is better than a dark room filled with the costliest furniture—more comfortable, more healthy, more enlivening to the spirits. Many people seem to prefer dim rooms. They hang curtains before their windows, and draw the window-blinds half-way down, and then sometimes fill up the remaining space with plants. These are rooms which bacteria must feel to be just meant for them. But we ought to be far too thankful for the light and its health-giving influence to shut it out in this way. Blinds are quite unnecessary things, and since they collect dirt they are much better got rid of. Even the plants, beautiful though they are, must be sacrificed rather than our rooms be suffered to remain dim. All that we need at our windows are curtains so arranged that they can be drawn right back during the hours of ordinary daylight, and drawn across the window at night, or during those few hours when the glare of the sun is very strong.

Artificial Lighting (Electric Light and Gas)

In a country like this, where the winter is tolerably long, it is also an important matter to have a good and safe artificial light for the dark hours. Any artificial light is more trying to the eyes than daylight and when it is very poor and dim it may do great damage to the sight of those who work by it.

Some people find electric light very trying; but, on the whole, if it is properly softened by a glass shade, it is the most convenient of all forms of lighting, and the most wholesome in that alone, of all artificial lights, it does not use up oxygen. It is used abroad more generally than with us, being much cheaper than here.

Gas comes next to it in convenience and cleanliness.

As far as possible ordinary gas-burners should be avoided and incandescent burners used. These last give a far better light, consume from 40 to 50 per cent less gas, and do not deteriorate the air nearly so much.

Where electric light is used great care should be taken as to how the wires are laid. If they cross one another there is danger of fire.

In the use of gas the danger to be guarded against is an escape of the gas, which may suffocate a person sleeping in a closed room, or may cause an explosion. On noticing any strong smell of gas, make sure that your windows and chimneys are open. Put a wet cloth over mouth and nose if you have to go into a room full of gas, and never take a light with you to see what is wrong until you have let in plenty of air, and provided plenty of means of exit for the gas.

Artificial Lighting (Lamps)

A form of lighting very commonly used is the petroleum lamp. If well managed this gives a very pleasant light, though it must be remembered that it also consumes a good deal of oxygen. If ill-managed it is both dirty and dangerous. Great loss of life is caused every year by accidents with lamps, and everyone should know what are the precautions by which accidents may be avoided.

The first thing is to see that your lamp is in order, and that each part fits into its place properly. The wick should quite fill the wick-tube—but not require to be squeezed into it. The chimney should fit well, so that it will not tumble off and all the parts which screw on to one another should screw firmly. When it is necessary to buy a new wick or a new chimney it is best to take the burner to the shop so that it may be accurately fitted. Wicks should be about ten inches long and after about two months' use should be changed. A new wick should be dried at the fire before using, and when dry should at once be soaked in oil.

The next important point is to keep your lamp clean in every part. Strictly speaking, the burner should be taken to pieces every day, in order to remove dirt and bits of burnt wick; this should be done, at any rate, once a week. The burnt crust on the wick should be removed with a bit of paper before lighting. Chimneys and globes should be rubbed clean with a **dry** cloth.

Next come one or two things to remember about filling the lamp. We must take great pains not to spill the oil in doing this. If any is spilt on the lamp we must wipe it away with the utmost care. The burner and the plug of the filling-hole—if there is one—should be screwed in tight when the filling is done. We should never have our lamp near a fire or near another light while we are filling it and we should never dream of refilling a lamp while it is burning. The oil-container should be kept **almost**, but not quite, full. Oil expands when heated, and will flow over the edge of the container if the latter is quite full. It is a bad plan to let lamps burn themselves out.

Before lighting a lamp we should make quite sure that it is clean and properly put together; and, in particular, we should see that the slit in the burner is exactly over the wick. Otherwise, the flame may touch the metal.

On first lighting, the wick should be turned down a little, and then in a short time gradually raised until the full flame is burning—but not so high as to smoke. If the edge of the flame is orange-coloured something is wrong with the burner.

If our lamp is not provided with an extinguisher, when we wish to put it out we should turn the wick down till there is only a flickering little flame. Of course, the wick must not be turned so far as to fall into the oil. Then we may put a bit of flat tin or card on the top of the chimney, or we may blow **across** the chimney—and the little flame will go out.

We must never blow **down** the chimney.

When a lamp is to be put away for any length of time, the wick should be removed, the oil-container emptied and stuffed with paper and the whole lamp wiped dry.

Colour for the Walls

A bright window, then, and sufficient light, are the first things we must look to in order to make our room cheerful; and next to them will come the walls, and the colour we choose for them. On the colour of the walls depends besides much of the prettiness of the room. On the whole, the two best colours are green for sunny rooms, and yellow for rooms where there is little sun. Yellow has been said to be a particularly healthy colour, much disliked by bacteria. It has a little of the exhilarating effect of sunshine. When choosing our colours, we must take care there is no arsenic in them. Arsenic is not found in greens and reds alone; it may be in any colour, and the papers and washes guaranteed as free from it are sometimes highly charged with this poisonous substance. The only way to be quite certain on this point is to get a chemical test applied to the colour.

Unless our rooms are fairly large they will be prettier if we have our walls plain. Papering is not nearly so good as a wash of distemper; and we should above all avoid flock-paper, on the surface of which dirt and disease germs will assuredly lodge. A yellow or soft green wash makes a dainty background for furniture and pictures, and when dirty it is cheap and easy to renew. Best and cleanest of all coverings for a wall is, however, varnished paint, as this can be wiped with a damp duster. Moreover, arsenic is not injurious in oil paint, as it is in paper or distemper, so that by using it we escape the difficulty of finding out whether the colour is arsenical or not. A dado of darker paint is serviceable in a room that is much used.

Carpets and Cupboards

Now we must turn to the floor. The worst thing we can do is to carpet it all over, as we saw in the chapter on bacteria. The best thing, after we have had the boards made tight if they were gaping, is to stain them and then varnish or beeswax them. Permanganate of potash makes a very pretty dark brown stain. This not only makes a floor nice to look at, but also easy to keep clean, as a beeswaxed floor does not need scrubbing or washing, but merely wiping with a damp duster. We may have a rug or two in each room, small enough to be taken up and beaten without trouble; we need nothing more.

Every house ought to be provided with good cupboards, for these are of great use in keeping things clean and orderly. They are much better built into the wall than standing out into the room as pieces of furniture.

Furniture

We ought to weigh carefully the necessity for each bit of furniture before we place it in our pretty, light, and cheerful rooms. Furniture means so much less air, and so much less light. No doubt we must have chairs enough for our family to sit upon, and one or two over for friends; we must have tables for meals and work, and shelves for books. But if we are sensible we shall refuse to cumber up our rooms with little three-legged stands, or bamboo tables that will only hold a photograph or two. Unless we have a really accomplished musician in our house, we shall certainly not give up precious space to a piano and as for stray easels, or odd chairs never meant to be used or drain-pipes draped with art-muslin, we shall very promptly clear them all away.

No people are so fond of crowding up their rooms with unnecessary things as are English people. Abroad the rooms are more bare and therefore look more spacious than with us, while if we go as far as Japan we shall find that furniture has practically disappeared, for there people sit on the floor to have their meals and so do without even chairs or tables.

At the same time, if we have but few things we should take some trouble about the choice of them, and see that they are good of their kind. Our chairs should be comfortable, our curtains and cushions pretty. In hangings and coverings fluffy materials should all be avoided, for the same reason that we should avoid flock-paper on our walls. We should use such materials as holland, linen, or muslin, which are easy to wash. These may be made very beautiful by embroidery, or by designs in another colour appliqued or stencilled on to them; and if we choose our colours to go with the colour of the wall we shall be surprised at the pretty effect the whole will produce.

By way of ornament one or two good pictures, one or two really pretty pots or vases, are much better than numbers of nicknacks, photographs, or bits of china.

Bedrooms

In the bedrooms the important piece of furniture is the bed. This comes long before hanging-cupboards, looking-glasses, or any other bedroom furniture. We should see to it that everyone in our house has a clean, comfortable bed. The best kind is a spring mattress with one mattress of hair or wool on the top. The worst kind of all is a feather bed, which is most unhealthy in more ways than one. A very good kind of mattress, which is also cheap, is made of the leaves of a sea-plant—known by manufacturers as *Alva*.

Our beds should be left uncovered to air for a considerable time every day. Abroad, as you go past the houses in the morning, you may see all the bedding hanging over the window-sills for the sun to shine on and the air to play over.

Beds should have neither valances nor curtains, nor should we stuff up the space beneath them with boxes—for the more air around, above, and below us while we are asleep the better.

If we can possibly manage it we should give each person in the house a separate bed, as this is by far healthier than having two or perhaps more to sleep in one bed together. Here again we may learn from our neighbours abroad; they never use the big double beds that we so often have in our houses.

Baths

A house with a bathroom was once a rarity; even palaces did not possess such a thing some generations ago, for we had sadly fallen away from the good old customs of the Romans, who esteemed baths among the great necessities of life. But we are steadily improving in this respect, and now very small houses, within reach of slender incomes, may be had with a fitted bath and a supply of hot and cold water.

No house should be without a bath of some sort—a fitted bath, a flat sponge-bath, a hip-bath, or at least a tub. Whatever it is, it should be in very constant use, for, as you know, we can hardly wash too often.

A very useful kind of bath is the vapour bath, the apparatus for which may be procured at no great cost.

Anyone who has not the opportunity of buying this may make a vapour bath by placing a hot brick in a pailful of boiling water and setting a cane-bottomed chair over it. The bather must sit upon a folded blanket on the chair, with another thick blanket fastened round the neck, and so arranged as to thoroughly cover the whole body, the chair, and the pail. After sitting thus till covered with perspiration, one should sponge all over very quickly with tepid water, rub the skin very dry, and then get into bed. Be careful not to use a chair put together with glue or the consequences may be serious!

Division of Labour in the Home

As we cannot have a healthy body unless every organ acts its proper part, so we cannot have a healthy and happy home if all who share it do not contribute something towards its welfare.

It is a bad plan for all the work of the house to be done by the mother or the sisters all the year round while the father and the brothers amuse themselves out of doors as soon as their work is over.

Girls and women need exercise and change as much as boys and men; in some ways they need them more, for their nerves are more sensitive, and they are more easily tired.

If one half of the family is suffering, the other half will assuredly suffer too; it is only when everyone takes his or her fair share of what is tiresome or fatiguing, and receives his or her rightful amount of wholesome pleasure, that the family can be vigorous and happy.

Whenever we notice that any person in our household is getting overworked, or is doing all the dullest and most monotonous things that have to be done, while others enjoy themselves, we should at once set about finding a remedy. On the other hand, if one or two in the household are having everything done for them, and doing nothing in return, we should put this to rights also; for if long-continued monotony and drudgery are bad for us all, so also is an easy-going selfishness.

Girls should have games and outdoor recreation such as boys have, and their brothers ought to encourage them and help them in organizing their games and clubs. Every man should be proud to have the women of the family bright and strong and energetic.

A very good rule to remember is, Never waste another's time. That means we should not be unpunctual, or untidy, or careless of our duties in our family life. One person's neglect in small matters usually means the sacrifice of another's proper rest or recreation.

These things make more difference than is commonly supposed to the health of a home, and they depend far more upon a knowledge of what is right, and the goodwill to do it, than upon any particular opportunities or advantages. If we once see clearly that a proper balance of work and recreation must be kept for everyone in the family, and have made up our minds that in our own family at any rate this shall be so, it will not be long before we contrive to bring it about. For where there is a will there is a way.

CHAPTER XIV

ILLNESSES AND SMALL ACCIDENTS

Nursing

"How much of the suffering of illness, as well as of its danger, is the fault, not of the illness, but of the nursing, is well known to the skilful physician and surgeon."

— FLORENCE NIGHTINGALE

JUST as all grown men and women, whatever their station or business in life, ought to know what are the right foods to use and how to prepare them in a simple, wholesome way, so, also, everyone should know how to get ready a sickroom and how to follow out a doctor's directions in such cases of illness as are not severe enough to require a trained nurse.

No one has done so much for nursing as Florence Nightingale, and her name will be remembered with gratitude by future generations.

The first thing to bear in mind is that what the body needs in health it requires equally in sickness, the only exceptions being exercise and kinds of food. Since in illness the energy of the body has to be expended in fighting the mischief, whatever it may be, it is usually desirable that the sick person should rest, and that the food given should be chosen for its digestibility or "lightness," quite as much as for its strengthening or heating properties.

If you will look back upon what we have said about the need of sunshine and air you will see exactly what a sick person needs; you have only to remember that those who are ill need more rather than less air, more rather than less sunshine, compared with those who are well.

The rules for personal cleanliness for washing the whole body over once at least every day, for brushing the teeth and the hair, and for getting rid of waste matter from the food-pipe—apply also to the sick; in fact, they should be kept with a more scrupulous care than ever. A person who is too ill to get out of bed and wash himself should be washed under a blanket in bed. Towels should be laid under him; the water used should be thoroughly warm, and the skin should be very carefully dried.

We have seen in a former chapter that a bedroom should be sparely furnished, and should have no fluffy hangings, nor yet a carpet covering the whole floor. This applies even more strictly to the sickroom. It should have nothing superfluous in it, and it should be kept as clean and fresh as the most diligent care can keep it. The bed should always stand out into the middle of the room, partly that the air may play about it the more freely, partly in order that it may be easy to get at both sides of the patient.

A sick person should, if possible, have a room to himself or herself, and should lie on a single bed rather than a double one. If two persons are ill at the same time, and it is impossible to give them separate rooms, they should, at any rate, have separate beds.

One point about the care of the sick, which is sometimes overlooked, is the necessity for frequent changes of bed-linen and of the patient's own garments. Nothing is more uncomfortable for the patient than neglect of this.

If there is anything in the room that requires emptying, it should be emptied **at once**.

In a well-kept, healthy house, care is taken to keep a fairly equable temperature throughout the day. This is especially necessary in a sickroom. Anyone who is acting as nurse must keep a watchful eye on the thermometer hanging near the patient's bed, and must make up the fire or shade the room or open the windows wider according to its indications. Sixty degrees Fahrenheit is about the right temperature; it should not rise beyond 65° nor fall below 55°. Sudden changes of temperature may in many illnesses prove very dangerous. It should also be remembered that nothing is worse for a sick person than a close, stuffy room.

Regularity and punctuality are great promoters of health at all times, and great care should be taken to ensure them in illness. In cases of any importance a chart or list of the times for food and medicine should be kept, so that nothing may be forgotten.

The washing of the patient, and the tidying and

cleaning of the room, should be done at a fixed time, and done as quickly and deftly as possible, so as not to fidget and irritate.

The comfort of the patient should be the first care of anyone who is nursing. There are ways and ways of carrying out the doctor's orders and of doing all the necessary things. The person who is most gentle, considerate, and sympathetic in ordinary life will usually make the best nurse; while one who is selfish, unobservant, and unfeeling will assuredly make a bad one, even if she is skilful with her hands and knows what to do.

Though a sick-room must necessarily be somewhat bare, it need not be cheerless. A picture or two, a vase of flowers (not heavily scented ones), a table by the bedside with such small objects on it as the patient may like to have at hand, pretty soft colours on the curtains and bedspread—all this will give it a friendly look: but most of all the fresh air, the sunlight, and the daintiness and cleanliness of everything will make it cheerful.

In very many cases it is a good thing for the patient to have some employment or amusement. Books, card games, conversation—sometimes such occupations as drawing or knitting—not only help to while away the time but also assist recovery by keeping up the spirits. The nurse, however, will watch carefully to see that nothing of this kind is allowed to cause excitement, nor yet fatigue. All exertion, even if pleasurable, must be proportioned to the patient's strength.

Another essential in the sickroom is quiet. Sudden

startling noises, whether within the room or without, should be most carefully avoided. Many people are much irritated by a buzz of conversation going on in a passage or an adjoining room. The sounds of talking and laughing, of hammering, or any other noisy work, any clatter on the stairs, or walking about in heavy shoes, should be avoided when there is illness in the house.

It may sometimes be necessary to leave a patient alone. On such occasions great pains should be taken to have everything that will be needed in the interval placed within reach, whether it be food, medicine, or anything else. Nothing should be left to the patient's memory or suggestions. It is the business of the nurse to think out and arrange everything. All articles of food which have to be left in the room should be covered. Boiled milk can be kept fresh by standing it in a basin of cold water and covering it.

When to Send for the Doctor

People are often more ill than they need be because they do not send for a doctor in time.

There are many troubles which sometimes seem less important than they really are, and may be the beginning of much harm.

It is almost unnecessary to say that no bad illness or injury should be treated without a doctor's advice.

Simple Illnesses and Accidents

There are, however, a good many small ailments and accidents which we should all know how to treat without calling in a doctor, and some cases where we should know how to act before the doctor arrives.

In dealing with these we must avoid the common mistake of supposing that the more medicine we take the sooner we shall be well. Above all, we ought *never* to take those quack medicines which we find advertised in so many magazines and daily papers. Many of them contain substances which do harm in the long run even if they appear to do good at the time. Besides, it is well to bear in mind that to be constantly taking any drug, even if it be the right one for certain emergencies, is a bad thing. The body itself, with its millions of cells, its many and active organs, and its ceaselessly flowing blood, is always working hard to get rid of what is mischievous and to strengthen what is weak, and often the main things needed are fresh air, rest, and light food, so that more energy may be set free to carry on the natural process of cure.

Cold in the Head—This is infectious. Therefore keep the patient apart from other people as much as possible. Anyone who is growing fast, or is not strong, should be made to stay in bed for a day or two, and kept in an equable temperature. Light food should be given. One of the best things to give as food in almost any illness is Benger's Food—made strictly in accordance with the directions on the tin. A cup of this, or of warm milk or cocoa, is a good thing on going to bed; and if the patient is kept indoors, hot barley-water, flavoured with lemon, or sweetened, may be drunk freely. The throat should be gargled with the permanganate of potash gargle described on p. 36. If the nose is very troublesome, and breathing difficult, let the patient inhale steam from a jug of boiling water, the head covered with a shawl. The steam should be inhaled by the nose, and exhaled by the mouth. After inhaling, exposure to cold must be avoided. For a streaming cold, old rags should be used instead of handkerchiefs, and burnt when done with. The hands should be washed frequently and the face bathed with warm water. Pinafores, aprons, or shirt-sleeves should never be used for the nose at any time.

Sore Throat—Never neglect a sore throat. Gargle frequently with the permanganate of potash gargle, or with a weak solution of boracic acid powder. Be sure that the food-pipe has had its proper daily riddance of waste matter. Keep the feet warm and dry. Black currant jelly and honey, or a little vaseline, will often relieve the soreness.

If the throat gets worse, or if, after a day or two of care, it does not get better, seek a doctor's advice.

Diarrhœa—This also should never be neglected. The first thing is to keep warm. Wear a knitted belt or a piece of flannel over the abdomen. See that the feet and legs are dry and warm. A little reflection upon what we learnt about the food-pipe will show you that fruit and vegetables should be avoided. Starchy foods and milk are good. They should be taken cold; hot foods and mixed foods should be avoided. If the diarrhœa is at all severe consult a doctor.

Diarrhœa in babies and very young children, and diarrhoea in the heat of summer, require medical advice at once.

Bleeding—Many people suffer from frequent bleeding at the nose. When this comes on the best thing to do is to loosen the clothes and lie with the head somewhat raised. A key or other bit of cold metal at the back of the neck, and cold water over the temples and the bridge of the nose will probably stop the bleeding. If it does not stop, you must call in a doctor.

Cuts—A cut should be carefully washed in warm water which has been boiled, and has a little boracic acid powder in it. If it is a slight cut, a bit of sticking-plaster may be stuck over it, and the whole protected by a clean bit of cotton or linen rag, or the finger of an old glove, if the cut is on a finger.

If the cut is a wide one the edges after washing must be gently drawn together and fixed in place by narrow strips of sticking-plaster with an interval between. A strip of clean old cotton or linen rag, which has been wrung out of boracic acid and water, may then be wrapped round it.

When once the wound is clean do not remove the clot of blood which forms upon it, for this helps the wound to heal.

Before dressing a cut, wash your hands thoroughly with warm water and soap, and then disinfect them by dipping them in a solution of boracic acid. Use a pair of pincers or sugar-tongs rather than your fingers wherever possible; and use a bit of boric lint, or rag dipped in boracic acid and water, rather than a sponge to mop the wound.

If the cut is in a place where it is difficult to make sticking-plaster fix, it may be wrapped round with a bit of pink boric lint wrung out in water, or with an old clean rag dipped in a solution of boracic acid.

New cotton or linen should not be used to dress a wound.

If you will turn back to page 175, you will see that I have already told you how to deal with deeper cuts.

Gatherings—No one should neglect a gathering, however small. If it is open, bathe it frequently in water as hot as can be borne, and which has a little weak carbolic acid or some boracic acid powder in it. The water must be boiled before it is used. Cover it between whiles with boric lint and a clean bandage. If it does not at once improve, send for a doctor.

If the gathering is not open, boric lint wrung out of boiling water should be applied, and a doctor consulted.

Insect Bites and Stings—We all know how painful is the sting of a bee or wasp, and how irritating are the bites of gnats, midges, harvest-bugs and other insects.

If a bee or a wasp has stung anyone the best thing to do is to suck away the poison. This should be done immediately, and the place then washed carefully in clean water.

Gnat-bites or other irritating bites may be soothed by dabbing Scrubb's ammonia on them. Tar lotion and tar soap are also excellent, especially for the very tiresome bites of harvest bugs.

Burns—The great thing to remember about burns is that the air must be kept from them. The best thing to put on a burn is oil or grease—*i.e.* salad oil, linseed oil, cod-liver or almond oil, or else vaseline or cold cream. Carron oil (equal parts linseed or olive oil and lime-water) is the most useful of all. The oil or grease should be smeared on strips of lint or rag about the breadth of the hand and laid on the burn, and then the whole covered with a thick layer of cotton-wool or flannel. Never break the blister of a burn, and give the injured part complete rest. It is also important to remember that a bad burn always causes shock, and that the shock will require attention as well as the injury. The sufferer should be kept perfectly quiet.

If a person's clothes take fire, the only thing to do is to lay him or her down on the floor, with the burning part uppermost. Sacks, carpets, rugs—any heavy object of the kind which is at hand—must then be heaped and pressed down upon the flames to stifle them—if wet, all the better.

If it is necessary to remove any clothing in order to dress a burn this should be done with the greatest care. Boots, stockings, or sleeves should be cut away. If anything has stuck to the burn cut round it with scissors and leave it; do not pull it off. Such a case always calls for a doctor's treatment.

Bruises and Sprains—A bruise may usually be left to get well by itself. If it is a very bad one cold water bandages may be applied to it, and it will be better to keep the injured part at rest.

A sprain is a more serious matter, for it is caused by the ligaments round a joint being injured.

Anyone who has sprained his foot when out of doors at a distance from home should bandage the foot tightly over the boot. If the bandage is wetted after being fixed it will be all the tighter. On arriving at home the boot and stocking should be taken off with the utmost care, being cut if necessary. If a sprain is not specially painful it is a good thing to rub the injured part with oil or vaseline. Remember it is the rubbing which does good, the oil is only needed to prevent chafing the skin. If this cannot be borne, cold water bandages should be used and if the pain is still severe these may be followed by hot fomentation. The injured joint must be allowed thorough rest till the pain is gone.

Fainting and Fits—When a person becomes unconscious and lies quite still, with a very pale face, place him flat on the floor or on a couch. If the latter is possible, let his head droop a little over the edge of the couch. Loosen the clothes about the neck, chest and waist. If in the house, open the doors and windows, so as to get all the air possible, and keep people from crowding about the patient. Fanning the face is a good thing, while smelling-salts, burnt feathers or vinegar should be held to the nostrils. On recovery give a glass of very hot water. If the unconsciousness is prolonged, a doctor should be sent for, and in the meantime hot bottles should be applied to hands and feet, and the body kept warm. No brandy or alcohol in any form should ever be given except by a doctor.

It is well to remember that a stuffy room, tight clothing, and want of food are among the causes of fainting. Anyone who faints often should ask the advice of a doctor.

A person may fall unconscious not from fainting, but in a fit of some kind. Then the face will often be red, while the patient may throw himself about with violence. This may be very serious, and a doctor should be sent for immediately. Meanwhile, the sufferer should be laid on a rug or mattress, all the clothing loosened, and everything against which he might strike or hurt himself moved out of the way. When he recovers consciousness it is very necessary that he should have rest for a considerable time.

Shock—After any severe accident, after a bad burn or scald, a fright or a fall, and sometimes on receiving bad news, people suffer from what is known as shock. This usually shows itself by a sensation of cold, and by shivering. The face becomes pale, breathing is difficult, and the body feels cold. Slight shock may pass off without any further treatment than quiet and rest, but any considerable shock may render a person unconscious, and may even cause death. The sufferer should be kept warm, if necessary in bed. Hot bottles or hot flannels should be applied to the feet and the abdomen. If he is conscious he should be given hot tea or hot milk, and as he gradually recovers great care should be taken to prevent anything agitating or disturbing him. Rest is absolutely necessary after severe shock.

Concussion of the Brain—A heavy blow or a fall on the head may cause a person to become insensible, being, as we say, stunned. A doctor should be sent for at once. Meanwhile the clothes should be loosened and everything done to give the patient as much air as possible.

It is important to remember that after *any* blow or fall on the head, though it may not seem very severe, nor cause unconsciousness, it is wise to lie quite still and rest for a longer or shorter time in proportion to the severity of the blow or fall.

Ambulance Classes

Ambulance classes are now held frequently in all parts of England, so that it is very easy for anyone to join them. It is well to be on the watch for such an opportunity, and to take prompt advantage of it.

All girls and boys who have read this little book with attention have long since realized that the human body is as complex as it is wonderful. They will readily see that it is the work of a lifetime to acquire the knowledge and skill necessary to treat any of the more serious forms of disease or injury. In all but very simple cases ambulance work and nursing consist simply in preparing for the doctor and in carrying out his directions. Provided this is clearly understood, it would be an excellent thing if all boys and girls went through such a course of training as the ambulance classes supply.

FIGURE 42 — CORRECT SITTING
AND READING POSITION

FIGURE 43 — INCORRECT SITTING
AND READING POSITION

FIGURE 44 — CORRECT WRITING POSITION

FIGURE 45 — INCORRECT WRITING POSITION

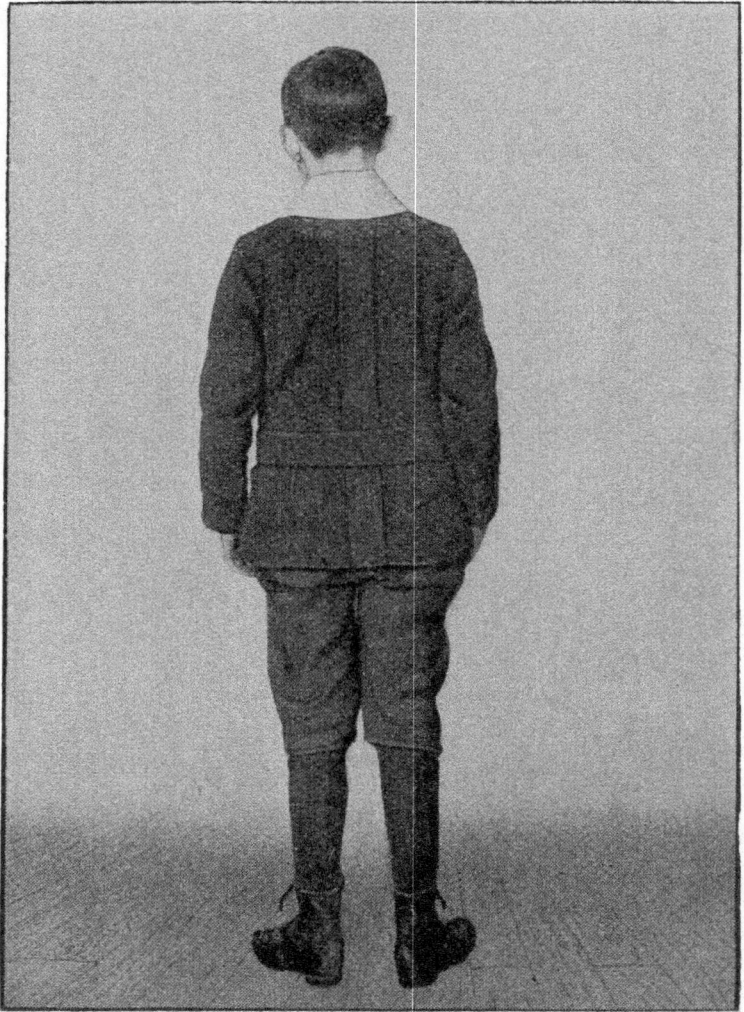

FIGURE 46 — CORRECT STANDING POSITION

FIGURE 47 — INCORRECT STANDING POSITION

APPENDIX

Breathing Exercises

N.B.—Clothing should be **quite loose**, and allow of easy movement of thorax, diaphragm, abdomen, and arms.

The best time to practise the exercises is the first thing in the morning and the last thing at night.

I

Stand erect with the head held easily, the shoulders back, the arms to the side.

1. Breathe in slowly and deeply through the nose only without forcing or straining.

2. Breathe out quickly and steadily. **There must be no movement of the collar-bones and shoulders.**

The same exercise sitting.

The same exercise lying flat on the floor or on a bed or sofa or table without a pillow.

II

The same as I, but when breathing in raise the arms sideways in a line with the shoulders, extending the fingers, the palms held downwards.

Breathe out naturally, and at the same time lower the arms to the sides.

III

The same as II, but when breathing in rise on heels, and when breathing out slowly sink.

IV

The same as II, lying flat.

V

The same as I, but when breathing in turn the palms quickly upwards and raise the arms until they are vertical above the shoulders.

Breathe out slowly and lower arms sideways and downwards.

VI

The same as V, but rise on the heels at the same time as breathing in, and then sink when breathing out.

VII

The same as V, lying flat.

VIII

Lying flat, with arms to the sides, breathe in deeply—hold the breath, count from 1 to 8, and breathe out rapidly.

Exercise of abdomen and diaphragm may be facilitated by placing some light evenly distributed weight on the abdomen such as an open book face downwards.

Postures

1. Sitting (Figures 42, 43, 44, 45)

The seat should be at such a distance from the floor as to allow the heels to touch the floor—with legs straight from the knee forming a right angle with the thigh.

The trunk should rest well on the middle of the seat.

The head should be held erect but easy.

The shoulders held back.

The spine arched inwards.

When reading and writing the desk should be sloped, and supported at a distance of not less than a foot from the eye.

2. Standing (Figures 46, 47)

The body should be held erect.

The head held easily, but not hanging down.

The shoulders held level.

The hips held level.

Both feet firmly planted on the ground, the weight of the body falling rather on the ball of the foot than the heel.

www.ingramcontent.com/pod-product-compliance
Lightning Source LLC
Chambersburg PA
CBHW032035080426
42733CB00006B/93